MEDEA

Psychoanalysis & Women Series
Series Editor: Frances Thomson-Salo

Feminine Sensuality
Alcira Mariam Alizade

The Embodied Female
Edited by Alcira Mariam Alizade

Studies on Femininity
Edited by Alcira Mariam Alizade

Masculine Scenarios
Edited by Alcira Mariam Alizade

On Incest: Psychoanalytic Perspectives
Edited by Giovanna Ambrosio

Motherhood in the Twenty-First Century
Edited by Alcira Mariam Alizade

Masculinity and Femininity Today
Edited by Ester Palerm Marí and Frances Thomson-Salo

*Women and Creativity: A Psychoanalytic Glimpse through Art,
Literature, and Social Structure*
Edited by Laura Tognoli Pasquali and Frances Thomson-Salo

*Homosexualities: Psychogenesis, Polymorphism,
and Countertransference*
Edited by Elda Abrevaya and Frances Thomson-Salo

*Myths of Mighty Women: Their Application in Psychoanalytic
Psychotherapy*
Edited by Arlene Kramer Richards and Lucille Spira

MEDEA

Myth and Unconscious Fantasy

edited by

Esa Roos

A volume in the Psychoanalysis & Women Series
for the Committee on Women and Psychoanalysis
of the International Psychoanalytical Association

Routledge
Taylor & Francis Group

LONDON AND NEW YORK

First published 2015 by
Karnac Books Ltd.

Published 2018 by Routledge
2 Park Square, Milton Park, Abingdon, Oxon OX14 4RN
711 Third Avenue, New York, NY 10017, USA

Routledge is an imprint of the Taylor & Francis Group, an informa business

British Library Cataloguing in Publication Data

A C.I.P. for this book is available from the British Library

   ISBN 9781782202912 (pbk)

Edited, designed and produced by The Studio Publishing Services Ltd
www.publishingservicesuk.co.uk
e-mail: studio@publishingservicesuk.co.uk

CONTENTS

ACKNOWLEDGEMENTS   vii

ABOUT THE EDITOR AND CONTRIBUTORS   ix

SERIES EDITOR'S FOREWORD   xi

INTRODUCTION   xiii

CHAPTER ONE
On the Medea fantasy   1
   Marianne Leuzinger-Bohleber

CHAPTER TWO
The ever present tragedy of Medea: women's   21
attack on their own creativity
   Laura Tognoli Pasquali

CHAPTER THREE
The age-old myth of Medea and the   37
Medea of Lars von Trier: the story of a woman's
love and compassion rejected
   Pirjo Roos

CHAPTER FOUR
Medea: maternal ambivalence   53
  Elina Reenkola

CHAPTER FIVE
Female destructiveness in fairy tales and myths   85
  Anneli Larmo

CHAPTER SIX
Sister fantasy and sisterly love   103
  Elina Reenkola

CHAPTER SEVEN
Conflicts around having two mothers: an interview   129
study with a Finnish war child
  Barbara Mattsson

CHAPTER EIGHT
On the psychology of love   151
  Esa Roos

INDEX   171

ACKNOWLEDGEMENTS

Chapter Six: A revision of a paper published originally in 2004 in the *Scandinavian Psychoanalytic Review, 27*: 12–19.

Chapter Seven: A revision of a paper published originally in 2011 in the *Scandinavian Psychoanalytic Review, 34*: 31–40.

Chapter Eight: A revision of a paper published originally in 2008 in the *Scandinavian Psychoanalytic Review, 31*: 77–85.

All these papers are published by kind permission of the *Scandinavian Psychoanalytic Review*.

Anneli Larmo, MD, is a training and supervising psychoanalyst of the Finnish Psychoanalytic Society. Director of the Training institute. Her doctoral dissertation is on how a parent's psychosis affects the family and children. In recent years, her interest has centred on sibling relationships, particularly depicted in fairy tales.

Marianne Leuzinger-Bohleber is a psychologist and psychoanalyst of the German Psychoanalytical Association (DPV), and the Swiss Psychoanalytical Society (SGP). She is Professor for Psychoanalysis at the University of Kassel since 1988. Since 2002 she is the Director of the Sigmund-Freud-Institute, Frankfurt a. M. From 2001–2009 she was Chair of the Research Subcommittee for Clinical, Conceptual and Historical Research of the International Psychoanalytical Association (IPA), and since 2009 she is vice-chair of the Research Board of the IPA. She is Visiting Professor of the University College London and Member of the Action Group for Neuropsychoanalysis. Her interest lies in clinical, conceptual and empirical research in psychoanalysis, developmental psychology, and prevention. She leads interdisciplinary projects with neuroscience, cognitive science, educational sciences and German literature.

Barbara Mattsson is a psychologist and full member of the Finnish Psychoanalytic Society, and a teacher and supervisor in psycho-analytic psychotherapy. She has given lectures on war children in Finland, Sweden, Norway, and London.

Elina Reenkola is a psychologist, training and supervising psycho-analyst and past co-chair for European COWAP. Her publications include five books on female psychology in Finnish *The Veiled Female Core* (1997, published also in English, 2002), *Female Desire* (2006), *Female Aggression* (2008), *Maternal Power and Strength* (2012), and *Female Shame* (2014). She has also written articles on pregnancy, breastfeeding, sister fantasy and female revenge. She lectures in many countries.

Esa Roos is a psychologist, training and supervising psychoanalyst. From 1996–1999 he was President of the Finnish Psychoanalytic Society; Director of the Training Institute from 2001–2007; representative of the House of Delegates of the IPA from 1998–2000; and past President of the Helsinki Psychotherapy Organisation. He was Consulting Editor of *Psychoanalytic Inquiry*, 1974–1977 and Associate Editor of *Psychoanalysis and History* since 1998. He has trained candidates from Finland, Russia, Estonia, and Latvia. Esa is Editor of six books on psychoanalysis and lectures in many countries.

Pirjo Roos is a psychologist and full Member of the Finnish Psychoanalytic Society and a group psychoanalyst who has written papers on films and Dostoevsky, and Lectures on literature and clinical issues.

Laura Tognoli Pasquali, MD, is a training and supervising psychoanalyst of the Italian Psychoanalytic Society, a Member of the British Psychoanalytic Society since 1976, and a Member of the Committee on Women and Psychoanalysis (COWAP). She is a group psychoanalyst and has presented a number of papers and lectures in Italy, Germany, and the USA.

I am pleased, as the Overall Chair of the International Psycho-analytical Association's Committee on Women and Psychoanalysis (COWAP), to write this Foreword for a new book in this rapidly grow-ing series. Otto Kernberg, when he was President of the IPA, set up COWAP in 1998 to explore scientific and political issues about the differences between women and men. A hallmark of COWAP is always being interested to engage with other organisations and ideas, and to open up a reciprocal discussion.

The chapters in this book offer a depth and breadth of creative and scientific interest, indicating work carried out over long periods of time. The writing is often poignantly evocative, fascinating, and powerful, whether to do with narratives around mythical Medea, or trying to find the meaning in a mother's murders that from the outside seem almost psychotic and to have lost touch with what is sane and real. The substantial core chapters and other illustrative ones widen the perspective to include painful implications of guilt and misery in relationships towards children, born and unborn, as well as the child perceiving the mother in a negative light or relating with ambivalent love, and where this slides over into the feelings of adopted children, or between siblings. The reader might not agree with everything written here, but is likely to be prompted to look again at what they do think.

On behalf of COWAP and its wider community, we are grateful to Esa Roos for the work in compiling this book from the contributions of a number of Finnish psychoanalysts as well as other analysts in Europe. The vibrancy of the chapters indicates that, as psychoanalytic thinking and work becomes more complex, our understanding of the analytic process is deepened, and with that comes a greater awareness of broader ways of understanding the field. I am impressed by the creativity that emerges from the fields studied and the ways of studying them, so that much that is new has been created in this book.

Frances Thomson-Salo
Overall Chair,
Committee on Women and Psychoanalysis

INTRODUCTION

Esa Roos

Our unconscious fantasies can be embedded in the age-old myths and legends. This book, taking Euripides' Medea as its starting point, is addressed to people who are interested in womanhood, its fortunes and misfortunes, creativity and destructiveness. When Jason rejected his wife, Medea, she killed their two children in revenge. Medea is known as both a heroine and a murderer.

Myths contain in condensed form stories which have interested people for hundreds of years. What can they tell us? What is the secret of their enduring presence? Jacob Arlow (1982) states that myths represent externalisations of unconscious wishes and fantasies in concrete form. According to Henrik Enckell (2002), metaphors in the form of myths help us to contact our emotions. Metaphor is seeing something in terms of something else (Ricoeur, 1970). Often, the unconscious comes closest to consciousness in the middle of tragic events. Aristotle's definition of tragedy was closely linked with the idea of catharsis: tragedy was an imitation of action and was enacted by characters on the stage. Compared to comedy, tragedy is usually more deeply affective. Breuer and Freud invented their cathartic treatment by using hypnosis. Sidney Tarachow (1964) regards the myth as one of devices which come to the rescue of the faltering ego. Myths ease the burden of ego synthesis and/or development and facilitate a working through of disturbing problems. There is an externalising and an internalising process. (p. 10)

According to Paul Ricoeur (1970), Freudian hermeneutics can be related to another hermeneutic, one that deals with the mytho-poetic function and regards myths not as fables, that is, stories that are false, unreal, and illusory, but, rather, as the symbolic exploration of our relationship to others and to Being (p. 551).

Marianne Leuzinger-Bohleber (Chapter One), when treating ten psychogenic sterile female patients in psychoanalysis, found unexpectedly that with all of them the way of experiencing their femininity seemed to be determined by the unconscious Medea fantasy. She also discusses the problems which abortion can cause for young women who are left alone without adequate help in the hospital.

Taking the Medea myth as her starting point, in Chapter Two Laura Tognoli Pasquali endeavours to outline the life of a couple where one of the two individuals abandons his/her own world to immerse him/herself in the other person's world. Tognoli Pasquali moves from myth to analysis to highlight a specific aspect of female masochism, characterised by tenderness and ferocity, violent aggressiveness and total dedication, which thrives in the woman at war with her own creativity. This kind of masochism has crucial social consequences in that it paves the way for perverse relationships between man and woman, master and slave.

In Chapter Three, Pirjo Roos describes the tragedy of Medea and its ancient roots and studies the film directed by Lars von Trier. She compares different interpretations of the ancient Medea story and focuses on the comparisons between the original drama of Euripides and the modern version of Medea by Lars von Trier. She studies the inner processes in the protagonist when love turns to hate and to a concrete plan of revenge.

Elina Reenkola (Chapter Four) examines maternal ambivalence in the woman's world, loving and hating the baby, and her attitudes and options in her entire life cycle. She particularly wants to emphasise the importance of the mother's law and the successive difficulties around the hate towards her. She discusses the phantasy of the murdering mother, Medea's shame and rage, and female ideals.

Anneli Larmo describes, in Chapter Five, the female fates of destructive impulses as they are illustrated in myths and fairy tales. She explains their making use of the death instinct and discusses its meaning not only in badness, but also in goodness. She gives concrete examples of myths of Medea as well as the famous fairy tales of Cinderella, Little Snow-White, Sleeping Beauty, and Mother Holle.

Elina Reenkola uses Edith Södergran's life and poems in order to focus on the unexplored area of sister fantasy in Chapter Six. She gives a clinical example of a young woman. The sister fantasy may serve as a bridge to separateness, and as a fetish to deny separateness and the feeling of insufficiency and not being lovable. In the close friendships of girls and women, the sister fantasy is present in a sublimated form. She also writes on the relationship of Anna Freud and Dorothy Burlingham.

Barbara Mattsson (Chapter Seven) describes the fate of a war child who had two mothers, the real (Finnish) one and the new (Swedish) one, and how she handled the conflict between them. She discusses traumatic reactions, feelings of emptiness, rage, shame, helplessness, and countertransference. After making the attack (of the USSR) upon Finland, almost 80,000 children during the years of 1939–1945 were evacuated to neighbouring Nordic countries, primarily to Sweden (72,000). 15,500 never came back.

In Chapter Eight, I write about love, saying that its essentially subjective nature makes it difficult to examine it objectively. Outlining the purpose of human life as the search for happiness and the avoidance of suffering, Sigmund Freud began the systematic study of the psychology of love. His most enduring contribution was the discovery of the link between adult and infantile love. Love is a strong motivational force in life and a central interest for all humanity. I examine what psychological factors lead to a happy result and what factors lead to failure.

References

Arlow, J. (1982). Scientific cosmogony, mythology, and immortality. *Psychoanal. Quarterly, LI*: 177–195.

Enckell, H. (2002). *Metaphor and the Psychodynamic Functions of the Mind.* Kuopio: Kuopio University Press.

Ricoeur, P. (1970). *Freud and Philosophy. An Essay on Interpretation*, D. Savage (Trans.). London: Yale University Press.

Tarachow, S. (1964). Mythology and ego psychology. Introductory remarks. *The Psychoanalytic Study of Society, III*: 9–12.

CHAPTER ONE

On the Medea fantasy

Marianne Leuzinger-Bohleber

Introduction

As Freud often stressed, unconscious fantasies are shaped in myths, art, and literary works in such a way that people of different cultures and historical epochs can relate to them, probably one reason why the organisers of this fascinating conference have chosen the myth of Medea as one approach to helping us understand in depth some aspects of female destructiveness.

For me, Medea, as an impressing, powerful, and passionate mystical female figure, turned out to be an unexpectedly helpful heuristic when I was confronted with the unconscious fantasy world of ten psychogenic sterile female patients in extremely intensive and difficult transference situations in their long and challenging psychoanalyses (Leuzinger-Bohleber, 2001). Briefly summarised, with all of these patients, the experience of their femininity seemed to be determined by the unconscious "Medea fantasy", which formed an unrecognised part of their own female self-representation. It was responsible both for the profound splits in their perception and experiences of their own identity as women and for their anxiety about their own unintegrated destructive impulses. Pivotal to the Medea

1

fantasy was the unconscious conviction that sexual passion carried the risk of existential dependence on their love partner, like Medea on Jason in Euripides' version of the myth. When she first meets the Greek hero in the palace of her father, Eros shoots his arrow of passion right into her heart; Medea has a presentiment of mortal danger and struggles with all her might against the overwhelming passion, curses the stranger and his appearance, but in vain. Having fallen in love with Jason, she fuses with him, helps him to tame the dragon and, thus, to steal the Golden Fleece. She then helps to kill her brother, who persecutes the fleeing couple. Her father, overwhelmed with narcissistic rage, tears himself to pieces. In the myth, the tragic fate of Medea that now ensues is the revenge for this double murder. All my analysands unconsciously were convinced that their love partners, in analogy to Jason, would deceive and abandon them and that they would not be able to endure such an abandonment and narcissistic injury. They were terrified by the unconscious belief that they would react to such a catastrophe with lethally destructive impulses constituting an existential danger to the self and the love object as well as to their children. As Medea had done, they would then kill their own offspring in order to take revenge. For this reason, it seemed to them psychically imperative to forgo any creative unfolding of their femininity and symbolically to "deaden" themselves and their bodies.

This fantasy system may, as Freud (1908e) presumed, have been an early infantile day-dream fantasy of the women, in which earliest bodily experiences and primal fantasies (as, for example, on the primal scene, birth and death, etc.) had been included and, as Sandler and Sandler (1983) postulated, probably was repressed into the unconscious in the fourth or fifth year of life, becoming part of the dynamic unconscious (see also Inderbitzin, 1989; Pines, 1993; Quinodoz, 1991). Today, we could talk about embodied memories of early and earliest object relation experiences, which are unconsciously enacted again and again in new relationships as well as, of course, in the transference (see, for example, Leuzinger-Bohleber et al., 2008; Leuzinger-Bohleber & Teising, 2012). They created difficult and sometimes even unbearable countertransference problems.

Thinking of the Medea myth thus proved helpful for me during many analytic sessions because the unconscious projections of the split-off, tabooed, murderous impulses of female destructiveness of my analysands on to me as their psychoanalyst in the transference confronted me with difficult and often almost unbearable counter-transference reactions, making it hard for me accurately to perceive and recognise this dimension of the "dark continent" of femininity of my female patients. To mention just one example from the psycho-analysis, which I will summarise a little later, after seeing my little eighteen-month-old daughter taking a bath in the garden, Mrs B, in the next session, recounted a detailed fantasy in which, beside myself with rage and anger after a quarrel with my husband, I cruelly struck out at my daughter and killed her. She would recount such fantasies in an oddly cold way, as if petrified and emotionally frozen. This evoked in me—as a young mother at that time—extremely negative countertransference feelings. In my struggle for visualisation and verbalisation of my overwhelming negative affects in such analytic sessions, the Medea myth helped me to create some kind of an inter-mediate space, finally allowing me to psychoanalytically reflect on this "dark continent of femininity".

Some commonalities in the biographies of the ten psychogenic sterile women

During the long and difficult treatments of these patients, it became evident that all of them had sustained severe traumas in their early object relations, with consequent excessive stimulation of archaic fantasies about the female body and characteristic modalities of the early relationship with the primary object. For example, it turned out that all these women shared the striking biographical fact that their mothers had suffered from severe depression and had been treated with antidepressants during the first year of motherhood. As a result, the mothers had presumably lacked an adequate capacity to present themselves to their babies as helpful, reliable, and indestructible objects that could have come to their aid in, for example, the progres-sive integration of archaic destructive fantasies.[1] The serious depres-sive illness of the mothers thus had impressed a powerful stamp on each patient's early self-development and the integration of archaic libidinal and aggressive drive impulses. In the meantime, not only clinical psychoanalytical studies are hinting at such tragic long-term consequences of early interactions with depressed or traumatised mothers: many studies in the field of empirical infant and attachment research have shown in detail and *in vivo* how influential such early interactions with depressed mothers are (see, for example, Amaniti et al., 2014; Lehtonen et al., 2008; Stern, 1995). In an impressive way Daniel Schechter (Schechter & Rusconi-Serpa, 2012) illustrated these insights in his paper at the last Joseph Sandler Research Conference: traumatised and depressed mothers cannot cope with a crying baby in despair because, unconsciously, the helplessness and acute pain of the baby reminds them of their own traumatic experiences. Often, these mothers leave the baby alone, which is, of course, a terrible experience for the helpless baby. Schechter showed a video of a little boy who entirely lost control of his affects because the mother had left him alone when he had suddenly begun to cry. Retrospectively, we found many indicators that the ten female patients I am referring to had gone through similar early traumatic object relations with their severely depressed mothers who were, by the way, German women, often equally traumatised during their own childhood in the Second World War.

The inadequate reactions of the traumatised mother make it impossible for the baby to learn how to cope successfully with his own emotions and impulses: he is unable to develop an early affect regulation and, therefore, integrates the archaic fantasies connected to such experiences which are, furthermore, associated with own impulses and needs. Consequently, these were preserved in the form of split-off, unconscious "Medea fantasies".

I have discussed the discovery and the working through of the Medea fantasy in psychoanalyses in detail in Leuzinger-Bohleber (2001). Within the frame of this chapter, I can only summarise one psychoanalysis, and I hope this will suffice to transmit an illustration of the clinical relevance of this unconscious "female truth". In the last part of my chapter, I shall just briefly hint at the fact that analysing the unconscious conflicts and fantasies of patients, often for several hundred sessions, not only offers unique insights into the specific unconscious world of these patients, but also, simultaneously, opens a window for current unconscious issues within our societies. One example is prenatal and genetic diagnostics, which provides us with the opportunity, and sometimes even the need, to decide on the life or death of an unborn baby, an external reality which always confronts us with the unconscious Medea fantasy, as I shall illustrate with an example from an EU-wide study on this topic.

*The unfolding of the Medea fantasy in the analytic process:
a short summary of a six-year-long psychoanalysis
with four sessions a week*

When Mrs B, a strikingly beautiful, fashionably dressed, thirty-year-old student, arrived for the first interview, her thick black hair and handsome, pale, somewhat lifeless, face reminded me of Snow White—an association that would resurface at the end of our talk when she told me that her father's death had abruptly driven her, a six-year-old princess, out of her infantile paradise.

In the following, some of the most important biographical facts, most of which emerged only after the third year of her analysis are briefly listed.

The patient's mother had lost her first husband in an air raid in 1945. She herself had been able to escape by running into a house, but he had been killed outside the door. After this, she had developed a severe phobia that had left her unable to work and caused her to lead a restricted life within the vicinity of her parents. She had met Mrs B's father in the early 1950s; according to the family tale, she had become pregnant the first time she slept with him and had given birth to an illegitimate, Down's syndrome daughter. Mrs B told me that because of this daughter's feeding problems, her mother had left her at the clinic, where she died a few weeks later.

According to the mother's narrative, a heavy burden had weighed on her pregnancy with the patient, as she had been very afraid of having another disabled child. The birth had been dramatic—a matter of life and death. It had, again according to the mother, been followed by a severe depression, for which she had been treated with drugs for eight weeks. The patient had hardly been breastfed, but had been fed in a "rigid four-hour cycle". When the patient was five years old, her mother had undergone a radical hysterectomy for a carcinoma. A year later, the patient's father had died. After his death, the mother led a withdrawn life at home, and neither pursued work in the outside world nor a new relationship with a man. The patient shared her mother's isolated life; having almost no childhood friends, she developed an infantile neurosis, which was never diagnosed or treated. During puberty, she still slept in the same bed as her mother, and her mother would read her diaries. A frightened Mrs B told me of an impulse she had had one morning to strangle her mother in the bed next to her. At the age of fourteen, the patient's phobia became so intense that she could no longer attend school, and she underwent psychiatric treatment with limited success. At the age of nineteen, her phobia made it impossible for her to leave her house and she was admitted to a clinic in Zurich as an in-patient. There she met her future husband who, finding this young woman attractive, had fallen in love with her. He was twenty years older than the patient, married her, and, thus, helped the patient to leave her mother. After the marriage, however, her symptoms caught up with her one after another; this had wounded her badly and ultimately motivated her to embark on a psychoanalysis.

I can only give an account of a few sequences of the psychoanalysis here.

During the first two years of treatment, she would often come in with dreams of an almost psychotic quality. To mention just one example, after I approached the oedipal dimension of her marriage in one session, she dreamt that she was looking out of the window of an ice palace, watching emotionlessly as some dwarfs outside fried parts of her husband's body on a giant grill. This dream reminded me of the Medea myths' sequence, where Medea first rejuvenates Jason's old father by cutting him up and boiling him under magic spells in a cauldron, and entices the daughters of Pelias to do the same with their father. However, to avenge the wrong Pelias had inflicted upon Jason's house, she knowingly passes on the wrong herbs, so that Pelias never returns to life (see, for example, Medea's history on the Pergamon Altar in Berlin).

The analytic work in these first years of analysis exposed the archaic anxieties concerning dependencies of Mrs B, which were due to the deficiencies in the formation of her self and object boundaries. Not only did this work lead to a loosening of the narcissistic defence and the associated substitute satisfaction, but also to a diminishment of her need to flee into a unique phobic world. This was followed, during the fourth year of treatment, by the appearance of the sexuality theme. To mention just one dream during that time:

"I am in our bathroom checking whether Mrs W [her cleaning lady] has cleaned everything properly. I lift up the lino and see some verminous bugs crawling out: I feel nauseated, squash these horrible creatures and am incredibly peeved that Mrs W did not do a better job cleaning."

During the second year of the analysis, Mrs B had repeatedly made the same conspicuous slip, calling me by the name of her cleaning lady, which had a variety of meanings: for example, feelings of triumph over, and devaluation of, myself. In association to the dream, Mrs B also mentions that her mother regarded sexual fantasies as "dirty" and they had to be "got rid of". Like Mrs W, I, as her analyst, was "accused" of not making such "unclean thoughts" disappear, but of taking an interest in them instead. Furthermore, during the ensuing sessions, it became clear to what extent Mrs B had also identified with her oedipal mother's "defective surgically mutilated womb". She said, "I have no feelings in this part of my body . . . it might as well be dead in there." After this session, Mrs B was admitted to the emergency room because of a presumed ectopic pregnancy. She reacted with severe panic attacks and resentfully reproached me in one of the following sessions: "Look what happens when we focus on this part of the body, I would rather go on anaesthetising my womb and keeping it dead."

A further topic emerged in the wake of the dream mentioned above: Mrs B associated the verminous creatures crawling out from under the lino not only with "dirty, male semen", but also with the children of her half-sister. During a recent visit, she had perceived the two children to be untameable, "crawling vermin". In the manifest dream, she killed off this "vermin" in a state of rage, something we could now see as part of the unconscious Medea fantasy, traces of something we were to encounter again and again during the following months. A vital element in the formation of this fantasy in Mrs B is the part of the family tale connected with the death of the Down's syndrome sister. Evidently, the analysand had later fantasised that her mother had "left the sister to die" in the clinic because she did not want her, because her disablement was a nuisance to her and wounded her narcissistically. In these fantasies, Mrs B experienced her mother as endowed with "power over life and death". Other sources for the stimulation of the Medea fantasy were fantasies concerning the female body which unconsciously seemed evident given the dramatic narratives of Mrs B's mother: pregnancy and birth seemed to be connected with catastrophes and death.

I cannot further describe how working through parts of the Medea fantasy again and again within the transference finally enabled Mrs B to enjoy sexuality for the first time in her life and, finally, to dare to become pregnant three years after the end of psychoanalysis. She called me several times during her pregnancy, as well as shortly before and after birth, because she still felt great anxieties and sometimes even experienced a few panic attacks. However, in the last telephone call, she proudly reported that she was able to experience the ups and downs of early motherhood within the first six months of her son's life to the fullest, without being drawn into the archaic abyssal maelstrom. As she characterised it, she was also able to discover herself, her son, and her husband as a "unique trio".

To summarise, while the traumatic quality of their early object relations had undoubtedly favoured the formation of this unconscious fantasy in the analysands like Mrs B, I now wonder whether the Medea fantasy might possibly constitute an ubiquitous unconscious fantasy of femininity. According to my clinical experience, it is observable in milder forms in most female analysands, because it is based on infantile sexual fantasies (e.g., oral fantasies connected with breast-feeding, as well as fantasies about the female body, pregnancy, and birth), and the frightening modalities of early object relating experiences with the maternal object. In this case, women (mothers) are not solely experienced as omnipotent givers of life who provide invulnerability and paradisical–orgiastic unification, but also as furies and avengers who, if wounded to extreme, extinguish the life to which they themselves have given birth. From my point of view, it is plausible to assume that, given a reasonably normal development, these archaic fantasies of femininity can be differentiated, cultivated, and ultimately integrated into a mature female self with a stable identity as a sexually active woman and good-enough mother. The knowledge of one's own potential destructiveness—which might, in an extreme situation, even be directed at one's own children—is psychically present within a stable female's core identity. Hence, a reflexive dialogue with the shadow side of one's maternity appears to be one of the prerequisites for an appropriate mothering capacity (including the holding function, containing, etc.), and for deriving mature narcissistic and libidinal satisfaction from it.

This hypothesis was further supported by clinical observations within the frame of a large extra-clinical study evaluating "normal" couples, not patients, in an extreme situation of their lives in which, due to an unexpected positive finding in the prenatal genetic diagnostics, they have to decide on the life or death of their unborn baby.

I presented a detailed report of this study at the last COWAP meeting in Berlin, yet I would also like to summarise some findings of our study mentioned in the last part of my talk, because of my introductory statement that the Medea fantasy, due to various achievements of modern medicine, has gained a new actuality.

Summary of the EDIG Study

Throughout a European-wide, multi-disciplinary study, we have thoroughly studied different facets of a relatively new field of medicine. The first result of this study have been published (Leuzinger-Bohleber et al., 2008; see also Fischmann & Hildt, 2011).

Achievements in genetic research produce ethical and moral dilemmas that must be a subject of reflection and debate in modern societies. The EU-wide study *Ethical Dilemmas Due to Prenatal and Genetic Diagnostics* (016716-EDIG), which was carried out between 2005 and 2008, tried to investigate these dilemmas in detail in a field which seems particularly challenging: prenatal diagnostics (PND). The existence of PND confronts women and their partners with a variety of moral dilemmas: should they make use of this technique at the risk of hurting the foetus through the technique itself and of possibly being confronted with the decision for or against the termination of pregnancy? Once they have undergone PND, data regarding abnormalities confront women and their partners with moral dilemmas regarding a life or death decision concerning the unborn child, the responsibility for the unborn child, for its wellbeing even with abnormalities, for its possible suffering, and so on. An important aspect is the conflict between individual beliefs and obligations and those of society's specific cultures. These dilemmas have not received full attention in our societies, creating a source of distress for women (and partners) that might be a burden on the relationship. Some couples show better coping capabilities, particularly if a competent professional's support is available. However, more research is needed to identify those vulnerable to psychopathology as a consequence of abortion after PND results, or of giving birth to a severely handicapped child. Pathology sometimes does not appear until years after the decision has been made. Our study was a step in this direction, but needs further, particularly psychoanalytical, research (see Leuzinger-Bohleber & Teising, 2012).

Following the EDIG study,[2] we are convinced that psychoanalysts, due to their very specific knowledge of unconscious fantasies, conflicts, and trauma, and as profound clinical experts, have something very valuable to offer to the multi-disciplinary and societal dialogue concerning these new and important issues. In a recent paper which was published in the *International Journal of Psychoanalysis* (Leuzinger Bohleber & Teising, 2012), we illustrated, through an example of an extensive single case, how psychoanalytic observations with patients during and after PND may, in a specific way, contribute to deeper insights concerning ambivalence in the context of modern technology and show how each individual who profits and suffers from it experiences it in their own very idiosyncratic human way. We tried to illustrate how psychoanalysis may be of great and long-lasting help for a patient coming from a genetically burdened family background. We also encountered similar experiences with crisis interventions for women during and after PND with a positive outcome, as I intend to illustrate shortly now (see, for example, Leuzinger-Bohleber, 2010). In the form of a liaison service with a large gynaecological clinic, our team at the Sigmund-Freud-Institut offers crises intervention for women/couples during or after prenatal diagnostics: one of the most important findings of EDIG was the following: women/couples who had taken some time and personal or professional support during the decision phase, working through the complex ambivalences connected with this situation and finally developed a certain feeling of "there is not a single good solution in this situation, every decision has its advantages and disadvantages. Nevertheless we have decided more or less adequately . . .", suffered statistically less frequently from depression and severe anxieties eight months after the decision.

Crisis intervention with a thirty-eight-year-old woman interrupting her pregnancy in the twenty-eighth week after a positive finding in PND

We are contacted by a senior physician, who asks whether we would be able to offer Ms E a crisis intervention talk: she had been admitted for a pregnancy termination and was in a desolate mental state.

I find Ms E in a single room of the gynaecological ward, a woman in her late thirties, alone and severely exhausted. She tells me that she has received medication to induce the termination and has been alone in this room for hours. The senior physician had promised to check on her but she has been waiting in vain. She was glad to have the opportunity to speak to me and had been informed about our offering.

Instantly, Ms E. begins to talk, although she is repeatedly overwhelmed by tears. She apologises. My response is "Let your tears flow freely, if you can—by God, you do have enough cause to cry . . ." Ms E was taken by surprise when a routine ultrasound revealed a possible defect of the embryo. "I come from a family without any history of disabilities. Therefore I had never considered not having a healthy child . . ." As a result, a triple screen test was recommended, which confirmed the diagnosis of trisomy 21. "My partner and I instantly agreed that we did not want a trisomy child . . ." Yet, both of them hoped that the amniocentesis would invalidate the diagnosis. "But it became clear that it was trisomy 21 . . . so we immediately made an appointment for the termination."

Ms E works in a management position for a well-known company. Her partner is also employed at this company. "We are both very strained with work—it would be impossible for us to care for a handicapped child. So it was clear we would decide in favour of a termination." The partner had already been fairly ambivalent when she had become pregnant. She, on the other hand, had been delighted, since her biological clock was ticking—she was already thirty-eight. "But maybe I had a notion that something could go wrong—I hardly told anyone that I was pregnant . . . And I was feeling so good. I wasn't having any troubles and felt entirely round and happy . . . The pregnancy was a counterbalance for the heavy burdens of home. My mother died two years ago and now my father is seriously ill. He is depressed. We had to send him to a home. Everything was up to me— I had to organise everything, and decide what was to happen to the large house . . . And now this . . . I had been so happily anticipating life with the child."

I hint at how unambiguous the decision to terminate seems. Ms E shows no signs of doubt. Therefore, I carefully enquire further. In tears, Ms E states, "Yes, we agreed right away. I couldn't possibly impose a disabled child on my partner . . ." During a longer communication phase, it appears evident that Ms E feels abandoned by her partner: "He had to work today and isn't even sure if he will come by in the evening . . ." "You seem very understanding towards him. And yet it would be 'normal' if you were also battling other feelings. The pregnancy is the product of your relationship with him. He is the father of your child, and yet it is you who must now carry out the termination. The child is a part of *your* body . . ." The fact that I mention negative feelings towards the partner, which are difficult to avoid in such a situation, seems to soothe Ms E. At this point, she is able to admit having an awful argument with her partner. "He reproached me for dramatising the situation. There are worse things. I should finally get a grip . . ." "This must have hurt you very much . . ." "I felt awful, I could neither sleep nor eat . . . Although I would like to go right back to work again, the entire situation is weighing down on me." I tell her about the EDIG findings mentioned above, showing the immense importance of the affected parties taking the inner and outer time to acknowledge and admit the scope of intense feelings associated to the decision in favour of, or against, a pregnancy termination, for the long-term coping processes. "This is about the life and death of your child . . . this is an existentially tough decision." Only after this could Ms E admit that she did not know what she was facing from a medical point of view. She felt insufficiently informed by the doctors. We go over the importance of her asking the doctor about the exact procedure of the coming hours, and that she should decide whether she would like to see the child or not, what should happen to the child, whether she wants to take pain killers or not, etc. The possibilities revealed through actively acquiring this information seem to relieve Ms E somewhat.

In the end, I ask her directly how she is feeling, whether she is scared of the hours to come, has feelings of guilt, etc. We are able to talk about her enormous fear of the unknown, especially the moment of birth. She is afraid the child might still be alive and she would have to watch it die. She is able to talk of fantasies and nightmares in which she carries an utterly deformed "little monster" in her womb: "Why am *I* not capable of having a normal child . . . My mother was past forty when she had me—I was a healthy child . . ." Again, Ms E starts crying.

At last she is able to admit to massive feelings of guilt. She grew up in a small village and was raised strictly Catholic. "Even contraception was forbidden . . . prenuptial intercourse as well as pregnancy termination were out of the question . . . Even though I did move far away and hardly ever go to church, oddly enough I considered receiving the sacrament of confession before the abortion or seeking out a priest . . ." Instead, Ms E sought out a consultation centre in the town. "The counsellor advised me to do what I consider to be right." In association, her thoughts repeatedly revolve around her mother's death. She reproaches herself for not having taken care of the cancer-ridden woman, but (instead) had gone on a trip around the world with her partner: Her mother died while she was still abroad. I ask, "Is it possible that you are harbouring irrational thoughts pertaining to the disability of your child being a punishment because you did not take care of your mother well enough?" Ms E stays silent, cries intensely, and, to my surprise, tells me she had dreamed of her dying mother the night before. "It was a fearful nightmare. I awoke and thought that least my child will be in heaven with my mother now." We talk about the resurrection of childish magical thinking in a situation such as Ms E is experiencing. The extent to which she is able to lament seems impressive: why *she* in particular must conceive a disabled child. "Sometimes it is easier to think of this as a punishment for something you have done than to bear the fact that it is simply unfair, that it can affect any one of us, to have a child with a chromosomal abnormality, just like that . . ." Afterwards, Ms E is occupied with blaming herself for not trying to become pregnant at an earlier age. "I was so concerned with my career and wanted a better life than the other women in the village . . ." I respond, "And maybe you are also experiencing guilt for that and have magical thoughts of being punished . . ."

Finally, we talk about the hours to come in detail and agree on the importance for Ms E of not being abandoned by her partner and at least to obtain some awareness of what lies ahead of her by obtaining precise medical information.

I give Ms E my mobile phone number and offer her the opportunity to call whenever it would be of any help to her.

Second crisis intervention session

Ms E calls me a few days later and requests a talk.

While crying, she tells me how very awful she is feeling. She cries for hours and feels very sad and depressed. She has had intense arguments with her partner, who yells at her and tells her to get a grip. I ask, "Is it possible that he cannot bear the thought that he is also accountable for your misery and in his view is unable to help you feel better?" Ms E reflects on this thought. She is experiencing strong feelings of blame towards her partner. She feels abandoned by him and blames him for the pregnancy as well as the termination. Hence, she is considering a separation and cannot conceive the notion of ever becoming pregnant again.

"He also avoided being there for the abortion. He did come by the previous night, but I noticed how uncomfortable he was and sent him away . . ." During labour, Ms E was "completely alone". She directs bitter accusations towards the medical staff because nobody was present when the contractions started. "Probably the doctors and nurses were just as scared the child could still be alive and they would have to watch it die . . ." I reply, "You were experiencing the same fear and so desperately needed someone with you . . ." Ms E is crying very hard while she talks about the details of the birth. Suddenly, the child was there and dangling by the umbilical cord. She did not want to look at it, but since nobody else was present she had to. "It was covered in blood—but other than that it was totally normal . . ." Finally a nurse arrived "and cleared everything . . . I was so distraught, as soon as I could I took a taxi and went home . . ." It was only the following day that she realised she had not said goodbye. She went into town, bought a blanket and took it to the hospital so that the child could be wrapped in it. Two days later she returned to the hospital and wished to see the child. The child had already been "thrown away . . . and they didn't use the blanket . . ." Ms E is crying desperately and expresses her anger towards the medical staff. "I wanted to tell you all of this, so you and your study can ensure that women in this situation are treated differently in the future . . ." Consumed by guilt, she tells me that she had signed a waiver stating that she did not want to bury the child personally. I encourage her to enquire again, since the child was most likely "not thrown away", but instead received a collective burial.

We talk about the importance, for her sake and that of the relationship, of taking the space to cope with her traumatic experience through professional consultations, and not, as planned, by plummeting back into work. She decides to seek out her former therapist, whom she had consulted a few times after her mother's death.

She thanks me for our talks and notes that they were very helpful.

Discussion and concluding remarks

In the first part of this chapter, I have tried to illustrate that the discovery (and the coping process) of the Medea fantasy was a prerequisite for Mrs B to give up her unconscious defence of psychogenic frigidity and sterility and to integrate her own female destructiveness into her female identity. This had been required in order to overcome her extreme fear of dependency on her love partner, to discover sexual passion, and, finally, to become pregnant.

With the second example, I reported some findings of a large EU study on ethical dilemmas due to prenatal and genetic diagnostics, thus mentioning a circumstance of our contemporary society in which all "normal" women may be confronted with the terrorising, unconscious Medea fantasies: for Ms E, as for all the women/couples of our study, the unexpected confrontation with a positive finding of PND, the necessity of deciding on the life or death of an unborn child, and, in particular, the experiences of late pregnancy interruption, were extremely burdensome. For some of them, they were even traumatic in nature (see Faimberg, 1987; Fischer & Riedesser, 1998; Laub et al., 1995; Oliner, 2014).[3]

As the crisis intervention with Ms E tried to illustrate, a woman going through such an emotionally taxing situation has to mobilise extreme forms of coping, together with defence strategies, in order to "survive" the acute (traumatic) situation. For psychic reasons, the complexity of the situation has to be radically reduced in order to enable a decision (e.g., deciding in just a few hours or days on the death of the unborn child). Therefore, it is unavoidable that this extreme situation in the external reality reactivates a corresponding inner "archaic" state of psychic functioning (see Leuzinger-Bohleber et al., 2008). As Freud (1926d) described, the confrontation with one's own death or the death of a close and beloved person (particularly one's own child) is an overtaxing psychic situation and absorbs all one's psychic energy at once, thus, mobilising relatively primitive defence and coping strategies.

The enacted archaic state of psychic functioning is dominated by a pre-ambivalent state of mind, which Kleinian psychoanalysts call the paranoid–schizoid position. This state of mind is, as we all know, characterised by an extreme psychic split between "bad" and "good", victims and persecutors. Connected with this state of mind is the reactivation of an archaic world of unconscious fantasies of murderers and innocent victims, witches and saints, devils and angels, etc. The Medea fantasy seems to be one such example of an ubiquitous female (body) fantasy.

From a psychoanalytical point of view, a confrontation with one's own unconscious archaic world of a murderous self and other can hardly be avoided when going through a late interruption of pregnancy, in which a "murdered child" is, indeed, part of "reality". This outside reality is often then confounded with the enactment of the "archaic inner reality". To get in touch with this state of mind and the archaic (of course, unrealistic) quality of the fantasies and its characteristic psychic functioning is a precondition for overcoming this state of mind, both during and after acute traumatism.

This means returning to a more mature level of psychic functioning where one can "rediscover" and experience the complexity and the ambivalence which are always connected to PND. This is indispensable in order to overcome the trauma or extreme crisis and to regain psychic health. This is one reason why a crisis intervention might prove to be of great help for women/couples in such an extremely burdensome situation.

Psychoanalysis, with its broad knowledge of trauma and the world of the unconscious, has a unique base of knowledge from which it can offer professional help to couples in such a situation.

Furthermore, taking up the critical view on culture from Freud on, it could also add an important dimension to the process of insights on the current actuality of the Medea fantasy in our contemporary societies. Sigmund Freud wrote, as early as 1930, in *Civilization and its Discontents* (pp. 91–92):

"These things that, by his science and technology, man has brought about on this earth, on which he first appeared as a feeble animal organism ... do not only sound like a fairy tale, they are an actual fulfilment of every – or of almost every – fairy-tale wish. ... Future ages will bring with them new and probably unimaginably great advances in this field of civilization and will increase man's likeness to God still more. But in the interests of our investigations, we will not forget that present-day man does not feel happy in his Godlike character.

Notes

1. These joint early experiences stimulated the unconscious Medea fantasy which is considered from the standpoint of object-relations theory because, as I tried to discuss in the clinical papers, it incorporates both early ubiquitous bodily fantasies and traumatic object-relations experiences. In the psychoanalyses, it proved just as important to establish a patient's individual split-off object-relations history, for example, by detailed understanding of the transference so as to bring out ubiquitous biological bodily fantasies. Progressive insight into their biological and biographical roots thus enabled me ultimately to discover and, hence, to moderate their unconscious feminine self-image, the "Medea-fantasy", a self image that is reflected in Jason's characterisation of Medea:

> Tigress, not woman, beast of wilder breath
> Than Skylla shrieking o'er Tuscan sea.
>
> (Euripides, 1910, p. 74f)

    Besides, all of the ten women discussed here did not only have in common extremely burdening experiences in their early object relations, but also in their preschool years. All of them had suffered near-traumatic losses during their oedipal phase (death of a close relative, such as father, mother, or siblings, dramatic divorces or accidents, or illnesses which could not easily be overcome). Another striking biographical analogy was the dramatic traumatisms in adolescence and late adolescence (see case of Mrs B).

2. The EDIG study offered a unique chance for a multi-disciplinary dialogue between ethicists, psychoanalysts, medical doctors, philosophers, and cultural anthropologists. It also described existing care systems across participating centres in Germany, Greece, Israel, Italy, Sweden, and the UK (see, for example, Raz, 2004; Ringler & Langer, 1991; Toedter et al., 2002, Wertz et al., 2002). Data was collected in two sub-studies. All the results were integrated into a discourse on ethical dilemmas. Study A recruited two groups of couples (positive or negative PND), total n = 1,687). Experiences with PND and related dilemmas were explored (questionnaires, interviews). Results were discussed in interdisciplinary research groups. Study B interviewed psychoanalysts and their long-term patients who showed severe psychopathologies as reactions to the dilemmas mentioned. Results of the study helped in discussing possible protective and risk factors for women/couples undergoing PND (see Leuzinger-Bohleber et al., 2008). In this chapter, I would like to present

just one of the extensive single cases in Study B in order to share our clinical observations with those of others.

3. If these experiences, as in the example of Mrs C, do have a traumatic quality, a specific coping mechanism, so-called dissociation, can often be observed: the self dissociates from its emotions, fantasies, and thoughts in an extreme way. It flees into a different state of mind that (on the surface) has nothing to do with the overwhelming emotions and fantasies in the traumatic situation. At first sight, the individual can function surprisingly well, is, for example, able to work and cope with everyday situations shortly after the traumatic event, as Mrs C did. However, at the same time, the individual has lost the inner connection to her self, her own emotions and thoughts, to the object (e.g., the partner) and to the "real quality of life". This state of dissociation is often not recognised by the person herself and is not connected to the traumatic situation: for example, to the loss of the baby, etc. As we know from long-term psychoanalysis, such dissociate states may sometimes endure for years and unconsciously determine the psychic reality of the individual. The severely traumatised person never finds her way back to "normal life" again, and never really lives in the present again. She has completely lost touch with the ground beneath her feet. She generally no longer feels any rapport with other people and has lost the basic feeling of being the active centre, the motor, of her own life (see also Leuzinger-Bohleber et al., 2008). For some of the women/couples this seems to be the case; even years after the pregnancy termination they have not regained psychic normality.

References

Amaniti, M., Trentini, C., Menozzi, F., & Tambelli, R. (2014). Transition in parenthood: studies of intersubjectivity in mothers and fathers. In: R. N. Emde & M. Leuzinger-Bohleber (Eds.), *Early Parenting and the Prevention of Disorder* (pp. 129–165). London: Karnac.

Euripides (1910). *The Medea*, G. Murray (Trans.). London: Allen & Unwin.

Faimberg, H. (1987). Das Ineinanderrücken der Generationen. Zur Genealogie gewisser Identifizierungen. *Jahrbuch der Psychoanalyse*, 114–143.

Fischer, G., & Riedesser, P. (1998). *Lehrbuch der Psychotraumatologie: Mit 20 Tabellen*. UTB für Wissenschaft. Munich: Reinhardt.

Fischmann, T., & Hildt, E. (Eds.) (2011). *Ethical Dilemmas in Prenatal Diagnoses*. New York: Springer.

Freud, S. (1908e). Creative writers and day-dreaming. *S. E.*, *9*: 143–153. London: Hogarth.

Freud, S. (1926d). *Inhibitions, Symptoms and Anxiety. S. E.*, *20*: 87–172. London: Hogarth.

Freud, S. (1930a). *Civilization and its Discontents. S. E.*, *21*: London: Hogarth.

Inderbitzin, L. B. (1989). Unconscious fantasy. *Journal of the American Psychoanalytic Association*, *37*: 823–837.

Laub, D., Peskin, H., & Auerhahn, N. C. (1995). Der Zweite Holocaust. Das Leben ist bedrohlich. *Psyche*, *49*: 18–40.

Lehtonen, J., Purhonen, M., & Valkonen-Korhonen, M. (2008). Des Traumas fruehe Wurzeln. In: M. Leuzinger-Bohleber, G. Roth, & A. Buchheim (Eds.), *Psychoanalyse, Neurobiologie, Trauma* (pp. 149–154). Stuttgart: Schattauer.

Leuzinger-Bohleber, M. (2001). The 'Medea fantasy'. An unconscious determinant of psychogenic sterility. *International Journal of Psychoanalysis*, *82*: 323–345.

Leuzinger-Bohleber, M. (2010). Transgenerational trauma: an unexpected clinical observation in extra-clinical studies. Paper presented to the Centenary Anniversary of the IPA of the Canadian Psychoanalytical Society, June.

Leuzinger-Bohleber, M., & Teising, M. (2012). "Without being in psychoanalysis I would never have dared to become pregnant": psychoanalytical observations in a multidisciplinary study concerning a woman undergoing prenatal diagnostics. *International Journal of Psychoanalysis*, *93*: 293–315.

Leuzinger-Bohleber, M., Engels, E.-M., & Tsiantis, J. (Eds.) (2008). *The Janus Face of Prenatal Diagnostics*. London: Karnac.

Oliner, M. (2014). *Psychische Realitäten im Kontext*. Frankfurt: Brandes u. Apsel Verlag.

Quinodoz, J.-M. (1991). *The Taming of Solitude. Separation Anxiety in Psychoanalysis*. London: Routledge.

Pines, D. (1993). *A Women's Unconscious Use of her Body: A Psychoanalytical Perspective*. London: Virago Press.

Raz, A. (2004). "Important to test, important to support": attitudes toward disability rights and prenatal diagnosis among leaders of support groups for genetic disorders in Israel. *Social Science and Medicine*, *59*(9): 1857–1866.

Ringler, M., & Langer, M. (1991). Das Wiener Modell: Ein interdisziplinäres Betreuungskonzept für werdende Eltern bei Diagnose "fetale

Missbildung". In E. Braehler & A. Meyer (Eds.), *Psychologische Probleme der Humangenetik* (pp. 123–138). Berlin: Springer.

Sandler, J., & Sandler, A.-M. (1983). The 'second censorship', the 'three box model' and some technical implications. *International Journal of Psychoanalysis, 64*: 413–425.

Schechter, D., & Rusconi-Serpa, S. (2014). Understanding how traumatized mothers process their toddlers' affective communication under stress: towards preventive intervention for families at high risk for intergenerational violence. In: R. N. Emde & M. Leuzinger-Bohleber (Eds.), *Early Parenting and Prevention of Disorders* (pp. 90–118). London: Karnac.

Stern, D. (1995). *The Motherhood Constellation: A Unified View of Parent–Infant Psychotherapy.* New York: Basic Books.

Toedter, L. J., Lasker, J. N., & Janssen, H. J. (2002). International comparison of studies using the perinatal grief scale: a decade of research on pregnancy loss. *Death Studies, 25*(3): 205–228.

Wertz, D. D., Fletcher, J. C., & Nippert, G. (2002). In focus. Has patient autonomy gone too far? Geneticist's view in 356 nations. *American Journal of Bioethics, 2*: W21.

CHAPTER TWO

The ever present tragedy of Medea: women's attack on their own creativity

Laura Tognoli Pasquali

I n the words of the protagonist Medea, "I least expected this terrible blow that struck me down and eats my heart, the joy of life, my dear friends, is lost for me and I only want to die. I have to admit my husband was everything to me and now he turned out to be the vilest man alive" (Euripides, 1985, pp. 225–230).

"I have to admit", says Medea.

She admits having devoted herself totally to a man who does not need her any more and now she sees, clearly displayed before her, her own predicament, the drama of a betrayed wife with no further rights in bed or, more importantly, no further rights in life.

Exiled in a hostile world that wants to get rid of her as quickly as possible, alone with her wild disposition and the terrible nature of a proud woman, the untamed granddaughter of the Sun God clearly and painfully recognises that she does not possess anything but the memory of what, in order to turn her husband into a hero, she has destroyed inside herself.

Medea's painful awareness extends dramatically from her personal situation to the wider and tragic social condition in which women are placed: discrimination, suffering, deprivation, oppression all gain meaning once they are thoroughly acknowledged. What is left is a deep sense of injustice expressed by a merciless statement: "Of all the creatures on Earth that live and breathe we women are the most wretched" (Euripides, 1985, p. 225).

The impact of this sudden awareness reaches such a profound emotional intensity that it cannot be easily understood or shared by one who has not experienced it or does not want to know.

The women's choral voice, listening to Medea, is only partially touched by her clear representation. The chorus feels pity for her and for itself, it sings desolate melodies and alternates them with a beautiful dream:

> Back to their source the holy rivers turn their tide. Order and the universe are being reversed . . . rumour shall change my life, bringing it into good repute, women's sex will be honoured and foul tongue's clamour sealed. (Euripides, 1985, pp. 155–158)

It sadly acknowledges that "time's long chapter affords many a theme on men's sex as well as on women's" and it tries weakly to console Medea. It is a cold, poor comfort that can hardly be credible: "Do not mourne for your husband's loss so much, be not angered with him, Zeus will judge and be at your side" (Euripides, 1985, pp. 155–158).

Medea's lucid awareness passed on to the chorus of women awakes an individual and historical conscience. This, however, soon dies out to a forlorn lament and this passive dream of emancipation becomes immersed in the false faith of godly justice once human justice has failed.

The women whose choral voice accompany Medea's humiliation can only delude themselves that the Almighty would grant them his protection. They cannot even denounce the painful injustice which they witness because they do not believe that "Phoebus lord of minstrelsy, has implanted in women's mind the gift of heavenly song" (Euripides, 1985, pp. 425–427); women must wait for a man to sing for them.

Like Medea, Silvia has been struck by unexpected misfortune. The man to whom she had completely given herself, her husband, has rejected her. Not because of another woman, but because she had become a stranger to him, she no longer amuses or attracts him. He feels tired, out of love, depressed, disinterested, and holds her entirely responsible for his state of mind.

All this happens apparently out of the blue, just in the moment Silvia is ecstatic about a much longed for pregnancy. Silvia feels desperate; she cannot understand. Exiled in her husband's territory, a husband who, by leaving her, takes away all her joy of life, she feels oppressed by a great solitude. Consciously, Silvia tries to react: maybe her husband is pouring his own malaise on her, maybe she has neglected him by being enraptured by the baby she has always desired and he has now become jealous . . . no, all this heaviness does not completely belong to her. It might even be that her husband is projecting on her his feelings of abandonment or is enviously attacking her creativity, yet, deep down in her soul, one voice that conscience does not control allows her to dream:

> "I'm sloppily wearing an ugly and shapeless brown coat, two friends are holding me and dragging me from one house to the other, ringing every bell. When someone answers, they open up my coat and, to the sound of a drum, repeat the same phrase: 'Look at this poor woman, her husband left her because she doesn't amuse him, look at her! Look at her!' I cry as they hold me up, unable to stand, slack, with no strength in me. Under the coat my clothes are even more sloppy, I'm wearing a long and baggy skirt and a grey jumper that covers up any form, my hair is dirty and my face is wet from crying.

> "The women keep repeating the phrase to the sound of a drum: 'Look, look at this abandoned woman . . .' People look and close the door again.

> "I reach an infirmary and manage to grab on to the nurse, who gives me a bottle of Grappa, telling me I need to get back on track with something strong. I withdraw because I don't drink, alcohol goes straight to my head. But the nurse insists, she forces me to take a sip and I feel a bit distracted from my pain."

The scene represented in the dream repeats itself obsessively during the night, like a nightmare, and Silvia manages, with a great effort, to wake up fully and not to fall back into the dream. She feels better, she tries to read until she dozes off and dreams again:

> "I'm in analysis, sitting in front of you, my husband is beside me and yours is beside you."

When Silvia tells me the dream, some days have gone by, the drum does not beat to the rhythm of her shame, and, even if still desperate, she is able to give me some associations.

The first scene reminds her of a flasher, an exhibitionist that once shocked and scared her as a child. It reminds her, too, of a dream where a woman would open up her raincoat and show two very big breasts.

The bottle of Grappa reminds her of something masculine and cheerful: having fun, drinking together. She is struck by the presence of only women in the first dream.

It is strange that, even if the dream is elicited by an abandoning man, it is inhabited only by women: Silvia wants to bring my attention to it.

Perhaps her husband has succeeded so well in projecting into her his feelings of abandonment in relation to her pregnancy because he had pressed the buttons of her own abandonment when, in Silvia's phantasy, her mother was exhibiting her new pregnancy.

Now, being abandoned by her husband leaves Silvia as helpless as a baby, so deeply hurt that she falls apart. Her internal support is represented by an experience of "good" breasts, her two friends, who hold her up and drag her from door to door to show to the shocked eyes of well-to-do people the true essence of a woman who does not attract her man any more: the living image of injustice. Under her coat, she hides a weakened, flaccid body rather than a fertile female womb and provoking breast. It is not a woman who mourns the loss of her partner, but an empty bundle of a baby that can only arouse pity. When she finally lands in the analytical shelter, she finds in me a nurse who does not show off her wounds, but limits herself to selling illusions that intoxicate her mind, rather than a mother who takes in how the baby feels. I get her drunk to strengthen up, to be more masculine, sing, be merry, directions Silvia finds difficult to swallow, and which, even if they temporarily distract her, she fears might hurt her rather than do her good.

Subtly, it is Silvia who is showing off my failure: "Look, look at this analyst, this narcissistic mother who would want to cure me from the humiliation of feeling absolutely impotent if abandoned by my man. She is showing off her breasts and wants to get me drunk with manic defences. But really she's a poor woman like me: without her man by her side, she doesn't function".

I must admit that what Silvia is saying carries some truth: to feel stronger and happier every woman needs to create a couple with a partner who respects and loves her. Unfortunately, this truth, pronounced in an atmosphere of misuse of power and exhibitionism, is thrown as a curse against women, disregarding the thought that men, too, need relationships of reciprocal dependence.

Centuries of history separate Silvia and Medea, but something also unites them. What is happening now has happened already. From century to century, different actors redistribute the roles, the costumes are slightly altered, the scenarios substituted, but the human soul's tragedies repeat themselves on the same stage of life with minor changes that are as slow as the course of history.

Two women, Medea and Silvia, are rejected by the hero that they themselves have contributed to shaping, a burning injustice that inflames Medea and extinguishes Silvia. A lamenting impotent chorus of women who expose the disaster and beat the drum of shame at the door of those who do not want to see and do not want to hear. False consolations that obtain a temporary dullness of conscience and, at the same time, a secret perpetuation of the tragedy.

In order to understand the drama, we should study its prologue.

Euripides conveys this in great detail: it is the story of a woman with an impetuous soul who has projected all her ambitions into her partner. She has lived for him, has allowed him to usurp her intelligence and abilities, for him she has applied her magic and seductive arts. To turn Jason into a hero, to allow him to obtain the Golden Fleece, Medea did not hesitate to kill the son of her own mother, to cut any bonds to her own past, and to go to live in the highly civilised Hellas, where she is considered a barbarian. There, in a world in which she feels a stranger, where she possesses nothing but the memory of what she has broken up, the dependence she has upon the hero she created is total, without limits. When Jason leaves Medea, being the granddaughter of the Sun God means nothing to her, and having that feminine sensitivity that originates in a deep involvement with nature's rhythms and mysteries, although it has given Jason more power and fame, has earned her the dangerous reputation of a witch.

Medea, this intelligent woman, generous and proud, so unlikely to put up with offence, has severed her own creativity in order to donate it to her life companion. In exchange for love, she has made his ambitions hers, she has thrown herself into avenging the offences he received, she has accepted his choices, his way of living. She denied her own family to be able to become part of his; she entered into the man's land, abjuring her own femininity.

Why? Why was she willing to give up her own self to worship the phallus?

I think we might find the answer in both the difficult condition in which women have been living (even psychoanalysis, as we unfortunately know, has not appreciated femininity much!) and in the narcissistic desire of being as potent as the worshipped man.

Before becoming a murderer in the play, Medea has already sacrificed her creativity for Jason: she has killed her own internal children to allow his to live.

The tragedy is already present in the prologue: the children she will kill in an excess of catastrophic and unavoidable rebellion are not Medea's, but Jason's children.

Silvia, too, is intelligent, capable, and generous. Even if she imagined herself with a chorus of women who emphasise her misfortune by showing off her nothingness, in fact, she has a beautiful feminine body and a lucid, acute, and intuitive mind. In her prologue, she fell in love with an ambitious teenager of many talents, a bit of an orphan, sent out into the world with only one sandal, but determined to conquer his kingdom, to become a managing director, a modern king.

She has always tried to soften any hard blows that might befall him, to protect him from any kind of fear, to prevent him from being hurt by feelings of depression, inferiority, or envy. Silvia has placed herself by his side and followed him in the many complex quests of his life and his profession. She has helped him to defeat his enemies and keep away the monsters that sought to prevent him from achieving power. She allowed herself a minimal space for the profession she chose and deluded herself into being happy to sustain his: she has denied her own creativity to fuel his.

In order to make her Jason feel great and powerful like a king, she bowed down to become the first humble citizen of his kingdom.

I do not think this type of masochism, which is, unfortunately, more common than we think, is just a female problem. I think it generates serious social consequences since it induces a perverse relationship between man and woman, between a false great hero who has everything and deserves everything and a foreign child-bearer full of resentment, guilt, and demands who lives in his shade and is full of admiration for him. It is a relationship that produces devastating results in which both individuals become victims: Jason and Medea, man and woman.

This relationship is caught by Euripides in the moment of its devastating break-up, when tragedy has become inevitable. When the woman, separated from the partner in whom she had invested all her qualities, finds herself deprived of any joy of life, of any ability to create, she becomes a monster "by nature little apt to virtuous deeds but most expert to fashion any mischief" (Euripides, 1985, pp. 408–409).

In the ancient scenario of the great theatre of life, a deeply divided couple locked in a mortal duel appears.

We can see a woman throwing back at her partner all those emotions she had carried for him, a wounded woman who inevitably is going to live and suffer until the very last breath a tragedy that has already been anticipated, a woman determined to kill the children that are not hers any more in order to claim them back and make the man also feel the desolation of infertility.

We also see a bewildered man too full of himself to be able to understand what is happening, a man passively subjected to an emotional storm he was not able to predict because he had always lived protected from any disturbing emotion. A man who is the victim of rhetorical thinking that has him accustomed to feeling sure of his intellectual and moral superiority to a point at which he is unable to see anything that is not in his own interest. A man who awakes in despair when all the emotions fall back upon him.

To be healthy, strong, and creative, a couple must be able to count on a true and real emotional bond that originates in the identification of a reciprocal dependence and a basic diversity. The joy that comes from giving makes the need to receive less humiliating. The pleasure of accepting is strictly tied to the security of having something precious to offer.

When the valences of giving and taking are reciprocally organised by the laws of interdependence, gratitude and love help greatly in tolerating the inevitable impulses of envy, disdain, and fear towards what is foreign and different and does not belong to us.

This is not just true between a man and a woman, but is true of all the couples where two different worlds meet and intertwine. When one of the two members gives up his self-esteem to find it in the other person, a very unbalanced relationship is established between the two, one of idealisation and submission, dominated unconsciously by envy and resentment: two ingredients that come into contact if there is a break-up and then have the power to spark off violence.

In the attempt to help Silvia and the many other women who, with different words and situations, present a common story to regain and value their own feminine attributes, feeling happy then with their own identity without having to get drunk on masculine identification, we must make the effort to understand how and why these attributes have been lost.

It is a particularly difficult task because the thread of the personal unconscious weaves itself so subtly in the socio-cultural cloth that there is a continual risk of remaining caught up in the attempt to discriminate between one or the other. However, maybe they are so intricately interwoven that it is not possible actually to separate them.

Psychoanalysis has taught us to reason in biological terms. Mysterious bonds link the mind and the body: the body becomes ill with the fantasies of the mind, the mind shapes itself on the body's pattern, but not only that of a single body or a single mind. The ripples spread out through a complex giving and taking scheme that pervades in an insensitive and concrete way through invisible, but nevertheless true, mechanisms. We can see the consequences, even though we might miss the details.

The mind cannot take any risks as it guides the body cautiously through the woods of reality. It looks for its piece of pleasure wherever it may find it, where it can get hold of it, in the most unthinkable places, competing with others, making alliances, settling on thousands of compromises.

The mind's adaptability is both its strength and its weakness. The freedom to think of things as they are, to say I like or I do not like this person, I desire this thing or I do not desire it, is a prerogative of whomever feels strong and confident and able to be himself. It is a rare fact, it is what in analysis we call *insight*, and when we find it we feel a thrill of pleasure.

"If I could admit to having been obedient like a dog," a patient once told me, "I could have been helped to be myself."

Are women poorer than men? "Not when they have a steady income and a room of their own", replies Virginia Woolf (1963), encouragingly, allowing us to understand with her imaginative and striking prose that income and room have to be intended as real and imaginary, internal and external spaces. While that might be true, it is really hard to fight against centuries of history, to enter the unreachable mechanisms of projective identification, the mysterious bonds between mind and body to reveal the light of that room that is already there: one must only be able to see it in order to own it.

Freud has always helped me, but now he is leaving me alone. I see him with his beard, that overshadowing genius, casting a curse on the race of women: "Anatomy is destiny!" I am scared of him. My first impulse is to deny everything, to say there is no difference between man and woman, but I get tangled up, I stutter, I feel like apologising and running away like a child who has interfered in an adult conversation . . . I shut my ears but his words keep resonating in me: "Even as a child, the girl considers her nature to be a fact and with this, the superiority of the male and her own inferiority" (Freud, 1931b).

Yet, the worst part is still ahead because, as I run away from Freud's voice, I hear a choir of women that follows me saying that the true essence of a woman is a man without a penis.

With this horrible image in my head, I ask myself if a woman will ever be free, proud, and happy with herself, or if she is bound only to accept the hard rock of femininity as a sad destiny of hers.

As I see the first female analysts walk by, Helene Deutsch, Maria Buonaparte, Ruth Brunswick, Lampl de Groot, my income shrinks down and the light in the room has reduced itself to a pinprick. I ask myself, "How could Medea follow her dreams and ambitions without living them through Jason? How can we help her not to kill her children?"

If whoever is talking about the moral, physical, and intellectual inferiority of the woman is a man, even if that man is my own father, my blood boils, but it is still me, I can rebel, defend my children, I can actually draw strength from them to claim my independent existence. But when it is a woman who utters the curse, I feel lost. They are right: the true essence of femininity is masochism, my children, and more so my daughters, are too weak to survive and I, who have inherited through this long chain of mother, grandmother, great-grandmother this bio-psychic inferiority, cannot do anything but submit to exile in the man's land.

If I am without that docility they assign to me, I will have to fight against a vengeful Medea, determined to kill the children of man to expose them to the desolation of sterility.

While looking backwards at my analytical parents, I feel I have understood a few things about Medea. I have understood it because Lampl de Groot is not my mother.

I have had a man as a mother (these things only happen in myths and psychoanalysis), son of rebel mothers. In my Kleinian house there lies a type of culture that allows me to have a room of my own and a fixed income, that does not make me run away scared by Freud, but it stimulates me to reason with him, contradict him, or even agree with him.

Anatomy is destiny and I am a woman in mind and body even if, taking into account those complicated crossed identifications of the mind and those chromosomes of the body that mix together and extend themselves and twist beyond the laws of probability, I believe I have a good part of a man in me, too. As a woman, with my female mind that has a piece of man in it, I am curious to embark on a journey in the obscure continent of femininity. After all, now that I think of it, it was Freud who advised me to do so!

I will start with Colchis, the mysterious place Medea abandoned.

Its earth is fertile and dangerous. It welcomes in its furrows the teeth of the dragon and it produces a human crop. It belongs to a magical world, populated by monsters, situated beyond the sea, thick with dark, secret, primitive forests, where reason has no tools to know, where eyes cannot see. It is a land dominated by forces that burst out primitive, unpredictable, intensely sensual, concrete, forces that work through unknown mechanisms that appear and disappear in precise rhythms that only an attentive wait can give meaning to. There are lunar forces that govern the crops, provoke tides, induce births, give the beat of menstruation. If reason does not possess the tools to know everything, if truth is hidden like the other side of the moon, intuition arises, extracting subtle perceptions and secretly connecting them until they are transformed into internal certainties that come and go but are never fully trustworthy. The unsettling, uncertain knowledge bound to precise internal perceptions, the curiosity of entering mysteries that nature has kept secret is an illicit power, fragile and precious. It is easy to blow it off, sail the sea to run to somebody else's home where everything is safe, clear, visible, and certain.

Yet, it is good to play and find what is hidden; children have fun finding secrets and if women allow them in, their house livens up with primitive, intense, and personal affection like the ideas that are nourished by them. I remember with great pleasure when Lucia, while recounting a dream, invited me into her internal feminine spaces:

"I'm in a strange room, which is connected to the outside by an opening that leads up into a narrow and long corridor placed vertically under the pavement. At the sides of the room are placed two winding stairs that I can't figure out where they lead to. With me a small girl full of curiosity wants to see my treasures, the objects of my childhood which I've cherished in a box under a tile in the pavement. The girl wants to see them all immediately. I calm her down, 'One at a time,' I tell her. She frees herself and, laughing, takes away something from me, maybe some small balls. She runs to hide among the columns the room is filled with and then down the corridor that brings her out to the outside. I laugh too, I'm not angry . . . I want the girl to stay beside me but she leaves. I know, though, she'll be back to get more balls and I will surprise and kiss her. I hide behind the door but the girl is smarter and faster than me, she takes advantage of the darkness and manages to run away from me again.

"The dream's atmosphere changes but the magic and intense emotion stay the same as I walk in the vineyards looking for a place which is known to me from my childhood and I want to find again. Colours, flavours, the smells of fruit are so alive and real that I can touch them with my eyes, mouth, and nose as if they were real objects. I look for my vineyard and it feels as if I can see the map of the hill I'm walking on from above.

"I want to make love."

In Lucia's dream, a girl is playing and a woman is having fun, while in the background there is a maternal hill filled with juices of heavenly taste. It is a feminine setting that describes minutely an internal anatomy that fills up with wonder: a dark uterine room, full of columns to hide behind, with its vertical opening towards the outside and the two lateral stairs that lead to a mysterious place, the ovary? and a happy girl, a phantasy of pregnancy? that plays hide and seek bringing down monthly the balls, the eggs? hidden in the treasure box.

Mysterious Colchis, the country in which Medea moves, is also a rich and fascinating feminine land. But it is scary, you cannot play there, there are too many oedipal monsters: a father who protects his great power from the greed of the young couple who want to take over, a mother who cannot defend her own son from the rivalry of her daughter, who cuts him up in order to run far away from her with a man who, adopted as a son, makes her feel as powerful as her father.

It is among these ghosts that Silvia and Medea move, blinded by their father's brightness, the son of the son of the Sun, and tragically deprived of a mother who should be able to give them strength, dignity, and desire to live. Silvia is barely supported by two women: sad and empty breasts with which she identifies herself. Medea runs from her dark and faraway motherland whose sons she kills to inevitably find herself killing her own.

It is among those ghosts that another tragedy unfolds, one of the most frightening of Euripides: *The Bacchae*.

Here, the king of Thebes, a virtuous and good-thinking leader, cannot even conceive the idea that women, mothers, even his own mother, could have the desire to leave the domestic setting and feel free to enjoy themselves together with other women. He struggles first to deny this possibility, then to forbid it, transmitting to us that ever present, alive, and current image, carved in tragedy, of the man in power who knows perfectly what is legitimate, moral, and good and imposes on others, often women, his orders and laws through the strength of his absolute beliefs.

For this powerful man, as well as for Jason, the massive falsification of reality has devastating effects. The splitting of the two worlds, male and female, the prototype of fractures and incomprehensions that we can continuously observe in the wider environment of relationships between different social groups, feeds through other splitting, subtler ones, more secret, more invisible, splittings that tend to deny dependency bonds and are extremely dangerous as they open the way to being overpowered. They are splits that create fractures between emotions and thoughts, making falsification indistinguishable from reality, splittings between perceptions and emotions that may eliminate any difference between desire and reality. Then justice becomes the dulling instrument of the strongest and power cannot comprehend the language of protest.

Whoever finds himself or herself in a situation of injustice can only run away or react with violence.

When our identity, our values, feelings, desires, needs, the true essence of our internal life, is denied and disowned to be substituted instead by ghosts created by someone else's desire, we must have a good dose of self-confidence to avoid becoming victims of insanity or masochism.

To be able to rebel effectively demands an employment of instruments and strategies that only the sufficiently rich can possess, certainly not those who have been impoverished by the massive denial of their own identity.

These considerations bring to my mind a remote place where women, and not only them, become always poorer, ghosts without a body and soul, forced into living behind a shroud that only a man can remove. This fills me with sadness and deep pity and makes me wish to go back home quickly, into my study, where I can do very little, just try to study this devastating need that humans have to possess the object upon which they depend and to try to understand why women become victims so easily.

By paying particular attention to the female transference and putting together disparate elements that repeat themselves with insistent regularity, it seems to me that we can become aware of the presence of an ideal mother modelled on desire that attracts the little girl, but then traps her in a deadly bond.

This is the ghost of a mother whose only precise task is to take care of the children: she feeds them and takes nourishment from them, has no interests, no sexual life, no internal project, no life of her own: a ghost who has created images of the sweet and delicate Madonnas our culture is filled with.

Unfortunately, our minds are full of them, too, but here, a much sadder picture appears: an empty, depressed, poor, anxious mother who is completely dependent on her husband and her children.

A particularly pitiful image for the girl who, on the one hand, wants to have a mother with no desires, completely dedicated to living for her, and, on the other, has to run away from such a sweet, dangerous ghost of a mother with whom she feels her own identity is bound.

I shall try to describe this weighty and anguished situation by opening the door of my analytical room at the moment in which Sara enters happily and gives me a book: a book she has managed to write and which has just been published. She gives it to me with a great smile, telling me she feels it is the practical result of our analysis: we are both touched.

The day after, however, Sara is depressed. She tells me, with sadness, that she is again demotivated, she feels alone, submerged by a heavy sensation of insecurity in her body as well as in her mind. I make a comment that Sara politely accepts, but I am aware it has not touched her in the slightest. Then she tells me a dream:

> "I'm in an art gallery with some friends, I stop to talk to them and I see Rita who, without a word, gives me a child who seems even smaller than it is in reality. I feel comfortable with people I know around me. Holding the baby in my arms, I lean on the wall, but I suddenly get sucked back by a cube of mirrors that twists and whirls and projects me to the outside in a place I seem to know well; there's an abandoned church and many ruins. It feels as if I've fallen back into the past and I feel lonely."

The cube of mirrors reminds her of Leonardo's labyrinth in which one can get lost through the insecurity of the reflected image. By entering it, one experiences a loss of identity, of internal, not external, space.

Sara livens up when talking about Rita, a poor woman she has been helping. Sara had given her money before, now she prefers to buy little things that Rita creates: bags, necklaces, and woollen sweaters. There has been a misunderstanding between them. Sara had given her a shawl to use as a model but Rita had sold it.

To me, it seems that the dream has turned into visual images the emotions that Sara had experienced and brought into analysis. From the feeling of being comfortably held among friends, she moved on to a situation of loneliness and depression, projected into her personal past scattered with ruins, a world similar to the historical Middle Ages from which Sara collects material for her books.

The change takes place through a loss of identity when she sees herself reflected in the analytical mirror that, because of a misunderstanding, distorts her image of herself and of me.

The exchange with Rita in the dream and in the associations repeats the exchange of the book. When she entrusts me with the book, she is afraid I might appropriate it and sell it off as mine: "Look at how good I am, how creative my analysis is!" and, on top of that, I entrust her with a baby that I should have taken care of. I steal her book, her creative ability to feel like a great, good, and capable mother.

At this point, she does not understand anything, her identity is crushed in a cube of mirrors where images change perspective so rapidly it is not possible to stop for an instant and understand all these aspects, hers and mine, that, without doubt, are present and are being reflected: her narcissism, mine; her gratitude, mine; my desire to want her to grow up, her feeling of being so small; her being an adult, my desire for her to be a child; my projections, hers. She looks for support by leaning on the mirror at her back, but my incapacity to hold throws her into a depressed world where it is difficult to work out who is doing the stealing and who is being robbed.

In the medieval atmosphere of her childhood, an abandoned church appears: here is a mother who had to keep her children small in order to feel like a mother, or is a daughter who, to grow into a woman, had to identify herself with a mother who does not have children of her own, but is carefully raising those of others.

The confusion is such that it feels like entering a labyrinth with no way out.

I would love Sara to allow me play with her treasures without immediately thinking that I want to steal them. I am sure that if she allowed me to play, she could forgive my narcissism and reflect herself then in the mirror of a mother who has her own girl to play with as well as an analytical daughter to take care of.

I notice I have gone back to the patient of whom I spoke earlier, to Lucia's dreams and to her maps to orientate myself and to find comfort. In her unconscious, there is a fertile hill full of fruit that stimulates an appetite for new and vital flavours: a faraway mother forever carved in memory, a girl who plays with the memories of a childhood jealously guarded in the most creative room of her internal house, a woman who dwells on a desire for birth that momentarily runs away, and a man who can be invited home to bring both pleasure and children.

I think this might be the map of a sane female structure, of a woman who has a room and an income of her own, a woman who can count on her own richness and can contribute to expand that of the man.

Summary

Taking Euripides' Medea as a starting point, I have endeavoured to outline a worrying area of the life of a couple when one of the two individuals abandons his or her own world to immerse him/herself in the other person's world. Determined to make her man into a hero, Medea does not hesitate to help him steal her land's treasure (the

Golden Fleece), kill her own mother's son, sever all links with her past, and finally end up in her man's highly civilised homeland, Hellas. Here, in a world where she is considered a barbarian, where she owns nothing but the memory of what she has destroyed, Medea depends totally on the very hero she has created.

Before appearing on the stage as a murderer, Medea has already sacrificed her creativity for Jason, has already killed her own "children" to live through his. The drama is in the prologue: the children are not Medea's, but Jason's, the ones that she kills, cruelly and tenderly, in a frenzy of a catastrophic rebellion.

I then moved from myth to analysis to highlight a specific aspect of female masochism characterised by tenderness and ferocity, violent aggressiveness and total dedication that thrives on the woman's warfare against her own creativity. A destructiveness that, as in the myth, originates in the past: the disturbing relation between a daughter and her depressed mother unable to defend her children from her daughter's rivalry. The daughter, whose identity as a woman is dangerously linked to that mother, tries forcefully to part from her, contributing with her departure to tearing to pieces her mother and her own internal children.

I support the idea that this kind of masochism has crucial social consequences in that it paves the way for perverse relationships between man and woman, master and slave, fake hero who owns everything and his child-bearer who, relegated to the shadows, admires him.

Jason and Medea, man and woman, are both the victims of this wasteful relationship founded on power rather than on love.

References

Euripides (1985). *Medea*, E. P. Coleridge (Trans.). Internet Classic Archive.
Freud, S. (1931b). Female sexuality. *S. E.*, *21*: 223–243. London: Hogarth.
Woolf, V. (1963). *A Room of One's Own* (pp. 156–158). Broadway Press. Encore editions 2001.

CHAPTER THREE

The age-old myth of Medea and the Medea of Lars von Trier: the story of a woman's love and compassion rejected

Pirjo Roos

"Without knowing what I am, and why I am here, life is impossible"

(Tolstoy, 1984, p. 823)

A remark by Sigmund Freud (1905a), alluding to the treatment of Dora in *A Fragment of an Analysis of a Case of Hysteria*, goes approximately like this: "No one who, like me, conjures up the most evil of those half-tamed demons that inhabit the human breast, and seeks to wrestle with them, can expect to come through the struggle unscratched".

With these lines in mind, so encouraging in their realistic stance, I try to approach the age-old myth of Medea, the drama of Euripides (480–406 BC) based on these ancient myths, and the modern interpretation of the story of Medea in the film by Danish director Lars von Trier (*Medea*, 1988). Lars von Trier is known for his many interesting and provocative films. (*Breaking the Waves*, 1996, *Dancer in the Dark*, 2000, *Dogville*, 2003, *Antichrist*, 2009, *Nymphomaniac 1–2*, 2013). This myth of the exotic princess and sorceress of the barbaric eastern kingdom of Colchis is an often cited, familiar story in our modern western world. Among many others, Freud (1905a) refers to her person in his writing of the analysis of Dora, with a short remark, to point out the circumstance that Medea allowed her children to be on friendly terms with Glauce, daughter of Creon, king of Corinth, despite all the troubles there were between the two women. Freud's remark is, perhaps, based on the resemblance of the drama of Medea to the complexity of state of affairs in the family of Dora and the very close friends of the family: there was friendliness and shared intimacy, but also many opposing, co-existing feelings of hostility and jealousy.

As is well known to the psychoanalytic reader, the treatment of Dora was interrupted prematurely, with Dora leaving Freud disappointed, maybe wondering what went wrong, with the feeling of having met unknown demons that had entered the scene and, thus, caused a premature interruption of the cure. Since the hoped-for positive results of treatment were not to be realised, one might be tempted to think that Dora was realising the role of "Medean" demon of the ongoing psychoanalytic treatment out of her wish for revenge. She decided to discontinue her treatment as she felt too hurt and humiliated when she found she was not understood properly. No doubt the many valuable insights that were born out of their work together were then lost for Dora.

However, for psychoanalytic thinking, this case has proved to be important, since it signified the turning of scientific attention to the importance, depth, and centrality of the daughter–mother relationship in female development, among other central concerns of psychoanalytic treatment (transference and countertransference): Freud survived the attack of the half-tamed demons and went on with his explorations of human mind.

The events of the story as pictured in the drama of Euripides

Medea, the exotic princess and sorcerer from Colchis, granddaughter of the Sun God, Helios, has been living with her husband Jason and their two boys in Corinth. She has been brought to this foreign country through her love for Jason. According to the old stories that form the basis to this drama of Euripides, she has been shot by the arrow of Eros, the playful but cruel son of Aphrodite, a god who causes uncontrollable passion in humans and enjoys the sufferings of the lovers, but never falls in love himself. A person, or even a deity, who is wounded by the arrow of Eros is, thus, destined be filled with uncontrollable desire. Medea has enjoyed high social status and security in her native country, but now that she has cut her ties to her own family, she is a stranger in Corinth, a world very different from hers. She has come from the distant East to the world of Hellas, a world that has left the primitive phases of its early history far behind. Medea has given up much, familiar terrain and familiar ways of relating to people and to gods. She is utterly dependent on her husband. She has escaped from Colchis, her home, with Jason whom she has helped to seize the Golden Fleece, the mythical, worshipped emblem of power. Medea's dedication to Jason and escape with him has brought great calamity to her family. The King of the city, Creon, has chosen Jason as his successor to the throne and has decided to give his daughter, Glauce, to Jason in marriage to seal their treaty and common political interests and ends. For Jason, this represents the longed for opportunity to gain power, therefore he accepts Creon's offer and abandons his wife Medea. Medea, rejected, deprived of all her future prospects, forced to renounce her marital position, enraged and humiliated, sets her mind on revenge.

She has left her own country and family for him, and helped him to obtain what he needed, the Golden Fleece. Now, betrayed and rejected by her husband and her new country, she finds herself totally unprotected. She faces a total change in her inner world: "But now hatred has corroded everything and dearest love grows sick" (Euripides, 1998, p. 1). She has to turn to the gods for help, mortals having betrayed her. Division into two distinctly separate worlds occurs: that of gods (grandfather Helios especially, but also the important feminine goddess, Hecate) with whom she now feels identified, and that of mortals, now a rejected part of herself. She rejects her identity as a mortal wife of Jason and mother of his sons: "I cannot but weep, old man—the gods and I planned all this, my evil plan" (Medea's line in Euripides). The process of Medea's joining with the celestial powers is much accentuated in Pasolini's interpretation of Medea: Medea finds in her crisis the basic coordinates of living and identity with the help of her mighty grandfather Helios (Pasolini, 1970). In Pasolini's interpretation, the central thesis seems to be that the new, developed world of Hellas has lost the capacity to understand the old world and its basic meanings and messages. Medea is, in Pasolini's analysis, the personification of an identity crisis. The sky and the earth are empty of old content and meaning for her in the new country: the sky and the earth do not speak to her there but remain silent. The basic coordinates of her life are lost. Only the regaining of contact with mighty Helios restores her lost identity and ability to act.

Pretending to have accepted her situation as a mortal, submissive, and rejected wife, soon to be banished from the country, she sends a gift to Jason's new bride: her nuptial crown and garments, letting her children bring them to her with their greetings and compliments. Glauce, young and innocent, unaware of any danger, receives Medea's gifts with great pleasure. The crown carries poison on its tips. Glauce is soon taken ill as a result of the powerful poison. Creon, the father of Glauce, in trying to help his daughter, is also afflicted by the poison and dies with her. The poison ignites their clothing and soon devouring fire consumes them both.

The revenge of Medea does not end there, but continues with the sacrifice of her offspring. The children meet their end at the hands of their mother, Medea. Her revenge upon Jason is, thus, complete. Medea leaves the scene in a golden chariot provided by her grandfather, Helios.

The murderess

The central thing in the myth of Medea is the death of her children. The reader is compelled to wonder why the murderous force of her hatred does not calm down after the killing of the bride and her father: why kill her beloved sons, Mermeros and Pheres? Even though "hatred has corroded everything and dearest love grown sick", why this terrible deed? In the drama of Euripides, the gradual growth and development of the murderous wish within the heroine and the inevitable direction of the impulse to turn finally on her own children forms one of the most impressive and frightening threads in the play. The process described by Euripides reminds me of *Crime and Punishment*, by Dostoyevsky: there, also, the psyche of the protagonist is slowly but surely invaded by murderous plans as a solution to his inner, tormenting dilemma (Roos, 1982).

Friedrich Nietzsche, examining the world of ancient tragedy in his early work, *Birth of Tragedy*, states,

But what does it transfigure [tragedy], if it presents the world of phenomena in the image of suffering hero? Least of all the "reality" of this world of phenomena, because it says to us: Look! Take a close look! That is your life! *That is the hour-hand of your existence!"* (Nietzsche, 1993, p. 114, my italics).

Sigmund Freud (1905b), analysing the character of Hamlet in his paper, "Psychopathic characters on the stage" (p. 308), says that this play of Shakespeare's, representing modern dramas, and being clearly a *psychological drama*, neither religious (rebellion against the will of the gods) nor social (rebellion against institutions) nor character drama (conflict between two strong individuals), is a description of psychological inner process in Hamlet:

> It has its subject in the way in which a man who has been normal becomes neurotic owing to the peculiar nature of task by which he is faced, a man that is, in whom an impulse that has hitherto been successfully suppressed, endeavours to make its way into action. (p. 309

In Freud's analysis he states further,

> (1) The hero is not psychopathic, but only *becomes* psychopathic in the course of the action of the play. (2) The repressed impulse is one of those which are similarly repressed in all of us, and the repression of which is part and parcel of foundations of our personal evolution. It is this repression which is shaken up by the situation in the play. As a result of these two characteristics it is easy for us to recognize ourselves in the hero: we are susceptible to the same conflict as he is, since "a person who does not lose his reason under certain conditions can have no reason to lose". [Freud quoting Lessing's Emilia Galotti]. (3) It appears as a necessary precondition of this form of art that the impulse that is struggling into consciousness, however clearly it is recognizable, is never given a definite name . . . (p. 309)

The course of the murderous action in the film of Lars von Trier

The terrible fate of the innocent children is something that audiences regularly find very disturbing. In the film made by Lars von Trier

(*Medea*, 1988), the act of murder is shown in minute detail. He has chosen that Medea will kill the children by hanging them: the smaller, resisting child she hangs with the help of her firstborn. After the baby is killed, it is the elder child's turn: he actually helps his mother to tie the rope around his own neck, with expressions of great devotion and compassion on his part. This is by far the most revolting scene I have ever witnessed in any film, and I would imagine that many feel the same. In a way, the boy is not a child any more; he is not in the position of a child protected by an adult, but has been made into a complicit peer. Jason comes to the hill soon after Medea has left and we are forced to witness the terrible scene of total destruction through the eyes of the horrified father. He sees the hill and the lonely tree and the listless bodies of his sons.

This scene that portrays the complete devotion of the elder son to his mother's cause brings to my mind Dreyer's film *Joan of Arc* (1928) and the saint's complete devotion to her cause, with its culmination at the stake.

The way the murder of the children is accomplished in von Trier's film differs from most interpretations of the story: for instance, in the film made by Pasolini (1970), the children die when happily asleep after tender goodnight kisses from their mother, unaware of the knife that ends their lives. We might want to ask here why hanging as a method of killing was chosen by von Trier and why he made such a long, harrowing scene depicting the event. Von Trier's Medea chooses a manner of execution that is linked typically to the masculine world of power. A more "understandable" way that I feel Medea, being a woman, would choose is to make use of her knowledge of poisonous herbs, or to use her own dagger, as in Pasolini's version. The von Trier way, however, accentuates the symbolic seizing of the ground of the masculine world and signifies the rejection of feminine in our heroine's inner world, something that Medea clearly expresses in the drama. Love and passionate devotion to her husband and caring for her children have proved valueless, and with the good inner image of Jason destroyed, the way forward for her is now only possible, it seems, by wreaking destruction, clearing away all obstacles in her path. Only this terrible deed can restore her lost sense of worth and enable her to regain her honour and self-respect.

The importance of self-respect to the ability to act and realise one's potential

In Tolstoy's *Anna Karenina*, we have an example of how important the feeling of worth and strong faculties of the mind are for the female characters: Kitty, wife of Levin, takes care of the dying brother of her husband and deals constructively with the painful situation of his imminent death:

> But Kitty thought and acted quite differently. On seeing the sick man she was filled with pity for him. And pity in her womanly heart produced not the horror and loathing that it did in her husband but a need to find out all the details of his condition and to remedy them. And since she had not the slightest doubt that it was her duty to help him, she had no doubt either that she could help him, and so she set to work without delay. The very details, the mere thought of which was enough to reduce her husband to terror, at once engaged her attention. (Tolstoy, 1984, p. 520)

So Levin, trying to understand her, could not but think:

> . . . She was in the same state of excitement, when reasoning powers act quickly, as a man before the battle, in conflict, in the dangerous and decisive moments of life – those moments when a man proves once and for all his mettle, and shows that his past life has not been lived in vain but has been a preparation for these moments. (Tolstoy, 1984, p. 524)

The film of von Trier is based on an original script by Carl T. Dreyer and Preben Thomsen, taken from Euripides' tragedy *Medea*. Carl Dreyer is known, for instance, for his film *The Passion of Joan of Arc* (1928). This Danish director is regarded by many critics and filmmakers as one of the greatest directors in cinema. So, for Lars von Trier, it must have been an exciting challenge to realise the script of his great colleague and countryman.

As mentioned above, in the film the death of the children is very much accentuated. When von Trier was asked why he had wanted to create such a harrowing scene, he simply pointed out that since Medea is really killing her children, it must be clearly shown in the open. In the terrible scene, the role of human hands, capable of both tender and cruel deeds, becomes evident in a very powerful manner. With her own hands, the hands that have caressed them lovingly, Medea murders her children.

About tragedy

The *Medea* of Euripides, on which the script of Dreyer and Preben Thomsen is based, is written in the spirit of the traditional form of tragedy.

What is demanded of a story for it to be called *tragedy*? There are certain rules for this. The philosopher Aristotle says in his work *Poetics* that tragedy is characterised by seriousness and dignity and involving a great person who experiences a reversal of fortune (*Peripeteia*). The change, usually from good fortune to bad, as in the *Oedipus Rex* of Sophocles (although it can also be from bad to good), is preferable because this effects pity and fear within the spectators. Tragedy results in a catharsis (emotional cleansing) or healing for the audience through their experience of these emotions in response to the suffering of the characters in the drama. Moreover, according to Aristotle, the reversal of fortune must be caused by the tragic hero's *hamartia*, which translates as "a mistake". This expression was in use, for instance, in the context of a spear thrower missing his target. So, it does not imply that there is any moral defect or flaw, but that a mistake of some kind has been made. The reversal of fortune is the inevitable but unforeseen result of some action taken by the hero.

According to Aristotle's definition, the causes for the downfall of the hero must reside in his own nature and not in any external powers, such as the law, the gods, fate, or society. In addition, the tragic hero may receive some revelation or achieve recognition about human fate, destiny, and the will of the gods: a change from ignorance to awareness of a bond of love or hate. The idea of catharsis is important in tragedy. Historians consider it probable that Aristotle has borrowed the term from medicine, and considered tragedy a spiritual kind of medicine, through which the mind is purified of certain painful affects (fear and pity), since it is these affects that are continuously tending towards discharge, thus causing painful feelings in an individual. According to Henrik Schück (1960), a Swedish historian and authority on ancient literature, it is *through* tragedy that they find the ability to make their "coming out" possible, almost as when an abscess bursts: the mind is relieved and the painful feelings are changed to feelings of enjoyment and pleasure: a very physical picture of the matter. This, Schuck considers, is how tragedy might be able to free us from the pain caused by real life. This understanding, dating from ancient times, of the importance of catharsis for the human mind links it also to our own science, psychoanalysis, and its early phases. As is well known, the idea of catharsis was substituted by that of free association for psychoanalysis proper.

The Euripidean tragedy is built on the older tragedy of Aeschylus. The young Nietzsche let himself picture in his mind the rationale: "thinker" Euripides meeting the older Aeschylean realm:

> And in doing so he had discovered what anyone initiated into the deep secrets of Aeschylean tragedy might have expected: in every feature, every line, he found something incommensurable, a certain deceptive precision and at the same time an enigmatic depth, an infinite background. The clearest character still had a comet's tail attached to it, which seemed to point to uncertainty, to something that could not be illuminated. The same twilight shrouded the structure of the play, particularly the meaning of the chorus. (Nietzsche, 1993, p. 58)

The young Nietzsche reproaches Euripides (Nietzsche, 1993) for bringing the elements of everyday marital conflicts to his *Medea*, and, thus, maybe losing or destroying some enigmatic depth that characterises the Aeschylean tragedy.

This enigmatic element that could not be illuminated or named has possibly found expression in Freud (1905b): "In the spectator too the process is carried through with his attention averted, and he is in the grip of his emotions instead of taking stock of what is happening" (p. 309). There, Freud displays the importance of the mental phenomenon of *repression* in an interesting connection: a psychological situation familiar to all of us when watching a theatrical performance.

The presentation of Medea to the audience in von Trier's film

The first scene of the film shows a woman lying in the shallow waters of the seashore, clutching the sand at the bottom, maybe to hold herself still, trying to resist the force of the waves. This scene then changes into a sequence of images of a strong whirlpool that surrounds and ensnares her, pulling her with compelling force from her initial position. Next, she is seen emerging out of the water, gasping for breath, heading towards the shore. This scene, I think, depicts her very interestingly. We spectators are faced with the mythical, age-old, mysterious heroine struggling for survival, coming into existence from the depths of the mighty seas. Thus she is born, the Medea of Lars von Trier.

The narrative starts at the point where the marital happiness between Jason, the adventurer and Argonaut, and Medea, his wife, is shattered. The harmony of the family is destroyed. Reliable and peaceful relations between the spouses have ended, and we are left with something that today we would call a broken home. Ominous signs of advancing catastrophe are depicted. We do not see the light of the sun; the skies are full of heavy clouds. These visual images convey the same message as the lines of Euripides: "But now hatred has corroded everything and dearest love grows sick". Lars von Trier's film-set calls to mind medieval times in the North lands. The landscapes are filmed in Jutland; the setting is dominated by the presence of the sea and long stretches of shore, inland slopes with long grass, bending in constant winds, and moist and damp lands. The palace of the king, Creon, the centre of power, is a gloomy, subterranean dwelling. The film itself, technically, is intentionally grainy and slightly overexposed, obscuring contours, leaving spectators uncertain about what they are seeing or not seeing. The interior scenes are full of flickering shadows. Torches on the walls of Creon's gloomy castle cast a meagre light on the surroundings. Outdoors, fog and rain dominate the scenes. In stark opposition to this obscurity is the scene of the morning of the day that will see the ending of the lives of Medea's sons. This crucial scene is filmed as a fresh sunny morning, full of sunshine and the sounds of a meadow waking up to a new day. Before events have reached this point, much has happened. All efforts to find a solution to the situation have failed. First, Medea declined to listen to Jason's arguments, then she implemented her secret plan of revenge. There was one attempt earlier by Medea to renew their liaison, but this ended in catastrophe. Jason brutally threw Medea aside, calling her a whore. Her plea to Jason to "remember" is rejected. The tender and sensual union between the two is over. The "dearest love" is not to be rekindled.

In the darkness of the night, Medea begins her painful journey to the place chosen to be the scene of the murder of her children, a lonely hill where a lifeless-looking tree is seen in the background. This painful walk has demanded everything she has. Von Trier's dramatic scene depicting this causes me to make associations to birth and a woman in labour (perhaps because of the laborious pulling of a kind of sledge containing the children up the hill), and thus to the painful and laborious, but ultimately happy, event of emerging new life. It also makes me think of the central scene of the Christian story: Jesus on his way to Golgotha. The film's audience is, of course, painfully aware of Medea's lethal intentions.

In the original drama of Euripides, the story ends with Medea being rescued in the golden chariot of her mighty grandfather, Helios. The ending in von Trier's film is different. In the film, Medea leaves the shores of Jutland in a boat belonging to her friend and supporter, the King of Athens, and is carried to the open seas by the rising tide. Then and only then, does von Trier show us Medea as a human being. She casts away her dark, tight headpiece and lets her hair flow free in the sea winds, the winds that soon gain strength and bear the boat quickly away. The expression of unswerving revenge that had masked her countenance during the tragedy is gone and she is shown as a woman, fragile and hurt. Expressions of sorrow are seen on her face, now that she is liberated from the awful task of exacting revenge. She seems to make a faint, hardly visible movement, as if to shrug off the terrible events and to wake up from a nightmare. Was it all a dream or a fantasy, the audience may wonder.

This resolution of the story is clearly different from the ending Euripides devised. At the end of his classical tragedy, Medea is carried to skies in the golden chariot. She joins the world of the immortals. The gods seem to take on the responsibility of the human catastrophe she has caused and been part of. Medea is liberated from it, and, unlike the male tragic hero, Oedipus, who is condemned to mortality and responsibility, sorrow, suffering, and feelings of guilt, she continues her existence untroubled, protected by divine forces, and goes on to life's new challenges (which include a new husband and new children, according to myths). Jason's fate was to be killed by the rotting hull of his ship falling on him while he was sleeping under its shade.

In Lars von Trier's version, the fate of the unhappy Jason is to be left as a wretched creature besieged by terrible winds; his lot is to remain a mortal stricken by terrible disaster. At the end, he is seen charging wildly around on his panicked horse. Jason is adrift. The aimless wandering of the erstwhile skilful and experienced sailor and Argonaut Jason calls to mind a vessel that has lost its anchor and is at the mercy of heavy seas.

In a way, the tragedy of Euripides could be seen as a story of the destruction of the ancient image of the "Aeschylean" hero, and, thus, an opening to a new, more realistic vision of man.

In his *Medea*, Euripides has given us a picture of a mortal, fallible man with all his weaknesses.

The *dénouement* von Trier offers in his *Medea* seems to be an effort to formulate and tie the story more to our own age, where the nightmarish events could be understood as our inner unknown "demons", dwellers in the unconscious layers of the mind.

The history of the myth of Medea

The interpretations and presentations of this age-old story of Medea, helpmate of Jason and murderer of her children, has had, as is well known, numerous predecessors, and the drama has captured human imagination for nearly three millennia, being the inspiration for many works by writers and visual artists.

Thinking of the many earlier versions of the myth, before the times of Euripides, it is interesting to note that, unlike most mythic figures, whose attributes remain fairly constant through mythology, Medea has a constantly shifting quality, being very far from a compact, integrated personality (like the masculine heroes of antiquity—Odysseus, for instance). In stories told of her she is an enchantress and a dangerous and independent priestess with secret knowledge over life and death, while, at the same time, she is also presented as a traditional handmaiden, a woman or young girl assisting and helping the hero through perilous adventures. But she has, undeniably, a very dark side: she is guilty of infanticide and fratricide, a murderess causing terror, destruction, and death. In addition to this role of destroyer, she is, surprisingly, also the founder of cities, thus an extremely respected figure, and, of course, she is, maybe most of all, *a foreigner*, the uncontrollable, the unknown one (Sarah Iles Johnston, in Clauss & Johnston, 1997, p. 14).

One of the reasons why the story of Medea is told and retold is probably because it is linked to the theme of the stranger. This theme has been important throughout the ages, and is still so in our own time.

The role of the outsider

When one tries to comprehend the situation of a foreigner and what it means to the individual who finds himself in the position of being an outsider, one is, no doubt, reminded of the fact that being an outsider results in a certain mental vulnerability and a position of unpreparedness as to what to expect; in a way such a person is like a child who does not yet know the rules. The outsider also often meets with hurt and rejection by those he lives among. The pain felt can be a challenge and threat to his mental balance, to his self-confidence, sense of well-being, and peace of mind. He might experience difficulty in defending his true identity. He must be continually on the alert and, because of his insecurity, he could develop heightened sensitivity and a sharper quality of consciousness, as well as greater investment in powers of perception. The newcomer often misses those moments of relaxation, joy, and shared pleasure that are available to those who are inside the protective net of society, to those who "belong".

Medea was a stranger in her new country, feared by the natives because of her alien nature and powers. As a woman, what would have been expected of her was adaptation to the values of her new environment, something that has been expected of, and experienced by, many generations of women entering their husbands' families. She was unable to do that owing to her strong personality. She is utterly dedicated to her awful task and brilliantly able to see her plan through to completion. She lies about her intentions with great success. Both Jason and Creon believe, naïvely, the sweet story of her good intentions, the older and more experienced Creon against his better judgement. She succeeds in her terrible plan with astounding ease: no barriers are raised against the evil deed; the men let her proceed with her revenge. The innocent children bring the poisoned gifts to the new bride, totally unaware of the mortal danger.

Medea is also a story of women and their situation in world of masculine order and power. Euripides gives us an excellent analysis of the situation that a woman with a will of her own experiences. Medea is deeply aware of the injustice she has suffered and is not willing to give up the awareness of being wronged. She accepts no blame herself for the catastrophe, even though Jason and also her trusted servants strongly suggest that it is her violent temper that is the cause of all the trouble.

Women, though they have always been able to form their own supportive groups, have long been denied education and have been kept largely ignorant of the experiences and lives of men, being relegated to domestic duties. They might have been able to take some part in the masculine world as muses or unofficial advisers, and also had some use as critics of those in power. This situation of having limited access to masculine fields of interest, while also being denied opportunities to act and take part as an independent authority, has created frustration, envy, resignation, and, too often, has placed women in the same position as that of a child denied the secrets of the "adult" world. This could have led to rejection and undervaluation of their own development and personality and idealisation of their husbands to a pathologic degree (Tognoli Pasquali, 2012).

Medea seems to resist aging: she is new to every generation and every generation is interested in her; her story must be told over and over again, with slight variations and changes of emphasis. The story of Medea contains elements that profoundly question our certainties about life and of the feminine psyche especially. Women are may be feared and felt to be "strangers", but they are not expected to act as Medea did. Shock comes from the realisation that the unexpected can happen; that women can sometimes turn out to be as cruel and dangerous as Medea was.

Lars von Trier's film ends in a very similar way to the original text of Euripides' *Medea* (1988) with these lines spoken by the Chorus:

> Zeus on Olympus dispenses many things
> and the gods bring many things to pass against our expectation.
> What we thought would happen remains unfulfilled,
> while the god has found a way to accomplish the unexpected.
> And this is what has happened here. (p. 38)

This concludes my treatise on Medea, a figure whose contours seem to change and allude to many things simultaneously. None the less, everything started with Eros's arrow and the uncontrollable forces it engendered when love first conquered her heart and then, as Euripides writes (in the words of the nurse, p. 20), "hatred has corroded everything and dearest love grows sick".

References

Claus, J., & Johnston, S. I. (Eds.) (1997). *Medea. Essays on Medea in Myth, Literature, Philosophy, and Art*. Princeton, NJ: Princeton University Press.

Euripides (1988). *Medea and Other Plays*, J. Morwood (Trans.). Oxford: Oxford University Press.

Freud, S. (1905a). *Fragment of an Analysis of a Case of Hysteria. S. E.*, 7: 7–112. London: Hogarth.

Freud, S. (1905b). Psychopathic characters on the stage. *S. E.*, 7: 305–310. London: Hogarth.

Nietzsche, F. (1993). *The Birth of Tragedy*. London: Penguin.

Pasolini, P. (1970). *Medea* (film).

Roos, P. (1982). Dostoyevky's "Crime and Punishment". *Scandinavian Psychoanalytic Review, 5*: 75–90.

Shakespeare, W. (1992). *The Illustrated Stratford Shakespeare*. London: Chancellor Press.

Schück, H. (1960). *Yleinen kirjallisuuden historia* [The General History of Literature]. Porvoo, Helsinki: Werner Söderström.

Tognoli Pasquali, L. (2012). The ever present tragedy of Medea: women's attack on their own creativity. Paper presented to Helsinki COWAP Conference.

Tolstoy, L. N. (1984). *Anna Karenina*, R. Edmonds (Trans.). Harmondsworth: Penguin.

Von Trier, L. (1988). *Medea* (film).

CHAPTER FOUR

Medea: maternal ambivalence[1]

Elina Reenkola

Ambivalence and conflict

Ambivalence means the simultaneous existence of two contradictory feelings or pursuits towards a person, thing, or situation. It often refers to the alternation of love and hatred towards a single object. Ambivalence is at the core of psychic conflict, as Freud (1915a) emphasised in his theory of ambivalent feelings. The alternation of love and hatred towards a single object is a neverending process, continuing as the basis of psychic conflict and leading to various defence methods and psychic solutions.

Early ambivalence can already be detected in a suckling. The infant sucks the mother's breast both contented and greedy, but disappointments and rage may arise, too. Sucking the breast brings pleasure, and disappointments with it arouse hatred. The infant also wants to bite the breast or swallow it whole. The infant wants to protect the pleasure-inducing, satisfying breast from its destructiveness and splits the bad breast off to separate it from the good breast.

It is both wonderful and distressing to be a mother, and a daughter. At its happiest, mothering may bring both deep joy and the feeling of fulfilment to a woman. The woman may feel that being a life giver and carer of her infant has brought new meaning to her existence. The "blessed state" of pregnancy may be seen as a self-sufficient mystery. For most women, however, pregnancy is laden with worries and conflicts. Becoming a mother shatters the woman's mind and body to the deepest core and raises early conflicts and longings related to her own mother to the surface. Pregnancy might ease access to the woman's central conflicts, making it possible to process them and work them through. This will then enable the woman's psychic maturity. On the other hand, becoming a mother puts a strain on the woman and predisposes her to mental disturbances. Motherhood causes conflicting and opposite feelings, that is, ambivalence, in the woman. Few European women nowadays feel that motherhood is the only satisfaction and fulfilment they can have in life. Mothers feel conflicting emotions towards their infants, and so do infants towards their mothers. Motherhood might feel as if it is a chance of self-fulfilment, but, at the other extreme, it can be experienced as forcing a woman to sacrifice herself and give up seeking more fulfilment in life; motherhood then feels like a prison.

Only a woman can experience how it feels to have a child develop and grow inside her as part of her in the symbiosis of growth and yet separate in identity. The experience of being bodily entwined might continue after delivery in the form of proneness to the feelings of symbiosis and the illusion of being one with the infant. This is where men and women differ, since men do not have a similar experience. They can, however, take upon themselves the maternal function (men-mothers) as Mariam Alizade (2006) describes.

Love and hate are influential powers in a human being. Mothers' aggressions have usually been passed over in silence. Mothers have often been idealised as Madonna figures, good throughout. It is difficult to accept the idea that mother, the giver of life, could be destructive and angry. Both mothers and children have difficulty in thinking about it. Yet, the wild beast of hatred lives in us all, requiring to be tamed.

The mother's ambivalence ranges from ordinary irritation or hatred towards a child who is making a fuss and refuses to be pacified to extreme cases. Then the mother might use mental or physical violence against her child, bully the child, or neglect the child's needs. The mother might use the child as a means of satisfying her own needs, sucking life force and encouragement from the child like a vampire. This seemingly special love and attention is, in fact, damaging to the child and not positive love that takes the child into account as a separate being.

One of the most shocking manifestations of destructiveness is infanticide committed by mothers. Mothers might also have murderous thoughts concerning their own children. Such thoughts cause boundless shame and guilt in a woman. The proportion of women committing violent crimes is but a small fraction, as men hold the clear majority. According to the statistics of the National Research Institute of Legal Policy, infanticide, however, is in most cases committed by the mother. Women are almost exclusively guilty of killing a new-born child, whereas older children could be killed by both mothers and fathers. Many women who have killed their new-born child have also been suicidal.

A hundred years ago, almost 100 infanticides a year were brought to court in Finland. Since the Second World War, after the increased use of contraceptives, the number of infanticides has decreased significantly. In the 2010s, statistics list about three per year.

A suicidal mother might take her child with her to death. She might be thinking that in doing so she is saving her child from a worse fate. In this chapter, I discuss a mother's anger and aggression as feelings and phantasies, not actual deeds.

Shame and pride are also powerful and conflicting feelings in a person. The vulnerable field of motherhood makes space even for shame and pride. A woman may feel intense pride when giving birth to a child, particularly if all goes well and there are no serious complications. An easy start with breast-feeding also adds to the mother's sense of pride, contentedness, and self-esteem. Shame, too, is readily present.

Life drive and death drive

Alongside love, every one of us carries the potential for destructiveness and aggression. Freud developed the concept of the death drive and its opposite, the life drive, or Eros, through various stages. Eros, or libido, means sexual energy, desire, and love. As our life drive, Eros strives towards wider connections and larger wholes. The death drive strives to dissolve connections and to destroy. The concept "death drive" describes the tendency to remove a disturbance and return to peace and a minimal state of excitement, as opposed to the erotic principle of binding. In the service of sexuality, the death drive leads to sadism. The death drive maintains itself as a quiet, numb force. Only when directed outwards does it appear as destructiveness.

These antagonistic drives of life and death always appear intertwined. Were the death drive to appear alone, it would lead to death.

Aggression is a manifestation of the death drive. Aggression refers to the attempt at harming or destroying oneself or some other person. It does not involve destructiveness exclusively, although it is often linked to it. It might also be a constructive force, necessary for defending one's boundaries, expressing one's own will, preserving the self, and even for kindling creativity. Aggression may take the form of physical or mental violence; it may harm another person, but also serve as a driving force for holding one's own.

Love and sexuality need aggressive energy as a driving force. Excessive aggressiveness would lead to confrontational, reckless, and cruel sexuality, with rape and sexual crimes as an extreme case. Too little aggressive energy in sexuality might make a man impotent, lead to prudence, submissiveness, overindulgence of his partner and giving up listening to his own will. Suppressed or insufficient aggression may turn the woman into a victim, unable to defend herself. If a person projects her or his aggression inwards, it might lead to self-punishment, depression, or, in its extreme form, suicide. In a woman, the sadistic aspects of the death drive do not easily become externalised, but tend to be projected inwards (Freud, 1920g).

Freud's death drive and conception of aggression may, alongside destructiveness, also act as a constructive force and help to define and defend the boundaries of the self. It may aim at self-preservation. Winnicott (1971, pp. 89–93) describes how, in order to be able to separate itself from the symbiotic love for the mother, an infant already needs aggression, the destruction of the mother, "symbolic matricide", as a constructive force. The infant destroys the mother, but when the mother survives the matricide, it becomes possible for the infant to experience her as enduring and separate. As constructive destruction, matricide becomes the background to real object love. The object of love, the mother, thus remains outside the infant's omnipotent control. According to Winnicott, an aggressive component is, thus, necessary for the infant to establish a separate external world. Aggression and "symbolic matricide" are also required in the oedipal triangle and in puberty, when a young person grows in tandem with the sexual adult. In youth, symbolic matricide is necessary for a daughter to be able to become independent of her mother and act as a separate subject. Symbolic matricide is also required for the daughter to compete with the mother in female society (Reenkola, 2002, 2004). Growing up is, as Winnicott (1971) says, inherently an aggressive act. In a girl, both love and antagonistic competition are simultaneously linked with the parent of the same sex, that is, the mother. For a boy, antagonism is directed more clearly at the father and love at the mother. The girl's unique position creates a particularly intensive love–hate ambivalence towards the mother. This moulds the fate of the girl's Oedipus complex and the vicissitudes of her aggression. Guilt-inducing oedipal competition with the mother may be further charged and empowered by earlier hatred towards the mother.

For the mother, aggression might be necessary for protecting her children and for self-defence. Aggression is essential in drawing boundaries for the children. It is sometimes necessary to forbid children things. All children's wishes cannot be fulfilled, and neither would this be advisable. For new life to be born, old life must be destroyed. Even in motherhood, giving birth to a new life, something old will paradoxically be destroyed; a woman is forced to leave her life as a single woman who could concentrate solely on her work and career (Reenkola, 2008).

Aggression may kindle creativity and provide it with the power it requires. The Russian psychoanalyst, Sabina Spielrein (1995), stresses destruction as the foundation of development and new growth, the birth of culture and art. She writes, "Where love reigns, the ego dies". Her writings on the death drive laid the foundations for Freud's conceptions. She is considered to be the forgotten pioneer of psycho-analysis (Covington & Wharton, 2006). Dmitry Olshansky (www.isfp. co.uk) describes her thoughts as follows:

> She is remembered in the history of psychoanalysis as the author of world-famous work Die Destruktion als Ursache des Werdens (her PhD thesis, 1912), which was basic for Freud's theory of death drive. In her thesis Spielrein puts forth for the first time one of the most difficult and important questions in analytic theory and practice, the question about the death drive, which arose through her research on maso-chism. There is an initial we-experience that is opposite to I-experience,

and that is related to destruction of the "I". At the same time, the destruction of the self and regression into we-experience has positive results, because it intensifies social development and cultural progress. She concluded that destruction is the basis of further development. In any dissociation, we can find a cause of becoming.

Spielrein's ideas are also depicted in the film *A Dangerous Method* (Cronenberg, 2011).

Dialogue between life and death drives is necessary for creativity to emerge, as Alizade (1999) states. Creativity always requires the breaking of boundaries, transgression, which again needs aggression to provide it with power. Hatred and vindictiveness may be processed in the mind symbolically, by means of phantasies and creativity. There will then be no need to progress to destructive action. Vindictiveness may also serve as a force or stimulus to creativity. It may take place symbolically with a creative work of art, verbal lashing, or the touch of a paintbrush (Reenkola, 2008).

Freud did not use the term Thanatos for the death drive in his writings. He was known, though, to use it occasionally in conversation (Laplanche & Pontalis, 1973). In post-Freudian thought, the death drive is sometimes referred to as "Thanatos", complementing "Eros".

Thanatos has been used as a concept by Ikonen and Rechardt (2010) in their interpretation of the death drive, where the removal of disturbance is emphasised as the prime objective of Thanatos.

Green (1999) uses the concept of the death drive in his writings on destructiveness, "the work of the negative". He describes how the destructiveness of the death drive appears above all as the psychic de-investment of the object. The aim of the destructiveness of the death drive is to unbind and strip the object of meaning (disobjectalising function). Besides object relationships, the death drive also attacks the ego, leading to its impoverishment. Stripping the object of meanings and investments appears, for instance, in melancholy, childhood autism, chronic psychosis, anorexia nervosa, and different somatic disorders in children. This is quite different from the step-by-step letting go of mourning; it is, in fact, its opposite, as it radically hinders mourning. The aim of the life drive is the opposite of this and involves the giving of meaning to the object. The objectalising aim of the life, or erotic, drives has the major consequence of achieving, through the mediation of the sexual function, symbolisation, which Bion, Winnicott, and Lacan have emphasised (Green, 1999, p. 88).

The ambivalent feelings of hatred and love belong to the core of a human being and produce conflicts and anxiety. Love and hatred, libido and aggression, come from different sources and each has its own evolution. Love is related to sexual desire. Hatred derives from the death drive or the struggle for self-preservation and solidification of the self. The concept of ambivalence allows us to keep the opposite nature of love and aggressiveness separate from the positive–negative dichotomy; love, as such, is not always exclusively positive or aggression negative. The striving of love towards a momentary fusion with the object may be destructive to the other's self. Love may be binding, stifling, or sadistic, a real power of destruction. Aggression, for its part, may be a necessary and constructive force. Both love and hate involve aggression, as Winnicott (1984) states.

The death drive may also appear as violence. Violence means causing damage to another person, violating their rights or interests, or using bodily strength to impose one's will upon them. Mental or psychic violence does not involve the use of bodily strength. Hatred is a subjective feeling, an affect born out of disappointments in the fulfilment of one's hopes and desires. When aggressive impulses are uncontained, the capacity of the ego for using symbols or words for them is threatened and this might lead to violent acts or turn them inwards.

My recent chapter (Reenkola, 2013) presented the view that:

> It is indeed true that women often express their aggressions indirectly. Sadistic impulses towards others tend to be turned inwards. One of the strongest motives for channelling aggression into indirect ways lies in the unique relationship between mother and daughter. In order to ensure the vitally important mother's love, the daughter will project her aggressions towards the mother to indirect channels or suppress them entirely. A woman might turn her aggressions on herself or use her children as an instrument of hatred and revenge. The invisible inner space, its pleasure and potential for interiority shape her experience of separateness and vicissitudes of aggression.

Love

Love is a profound feeling of passionate affection and emotion. We can talk about primary love, narcissistic love, primitive love, ideal love, sexual love, object love, or ambivalent love. We usually think of considerate love, but love can be inconsiderate and unconcerned about the other. Freud does not define love, although he writes about the psychology of love. He distinguished three types of love: anaclitic, narcissistic, and genital.

Healthy love gives as much, or even more, to the lover as to the loved one. The poets have known this, and Shakespeare (2011) has Juliet say:

> My bounty is as boundless as the sea,
> My love as deep; the more I give to thee,
> The more I have, for both are infinite.
>
> (ll. 133–135)

When does love begin? Is it a mystery? Early love of the mother already begins to manifest itself immediately after birth in the symbiotic relation with the mother. It begins in the first experiences of pleasure at the moment of feeding when the infant's hunger is satisfied and distress alleviated. Love and concern will develop in loving and solicitous relationships. Freud (1905d) wrote, how "a child sucking at his mother's breast has become the prototype of every relation of love" (p. 222).

Esa Roos (2008) writes about love:

> It is a fact that pleasure exists and rules the beginning of any kind of love relationships. Civilization fails to bring the happiness we expect from it, and without love, man cannot survive. Every man must find for himself the object of love to whom he can direct his need for affectionate attachment and for binding his sensual and sexual passion. (p. 78)

The love described in the Bible is the ideal love of a mother for her child. In "Letters to the Corinthians", love is idealised, purely good, and always considerate of the other person.

> Love suffers long and is kind; love does not envy; love does not parade itself, is not puffed up; does not behave rudely, does not seek its own, is not provoked, thinks no evil; does not rejoice in iniquity, but rejoices in the truth; bears all things, believes all things, hopes all things, endures all things.

Primary love is comprehensive and undifferentiated by nature, as psychoanalyst Michael Balint (1952) has described. The infant desires the satisfaction of hunger and love self-centredly and wordlessly, without the obligation of reciprocity. The infant is completely helpless and dependent on the mother; without care, nurturing, and love the infant dies. Pleasure and distress alternate in the infant's experience right from the start. Primary love begins in the infant with the experiences of pleasure, as soon as breast-feeding begins and hunger is satisfied. The early love relationship with the mother is for the child the prototype of love relationships in later life and reflects in the manner in which a person loves as an adult.

Primitive love reigns at the very beginning of the life, according to Winnicott (1990). He describes how primitive love is ruthlessly demanding. The infant's excited love includes an imaginative attack on the mother's body. This unconcerned demand evokes the hatred of the mother. He lists eighteen powerful reasons why the mother ordinarily hates her infant and they are all the consequence of the infant's ruthless use of her in the service of its own development. Optimally, she must not retaliate, but let herself to be used by the infant in the service of the developmental process. From the infant's point of view, he or she is simply loving the mother; from the mother's point of view, it can feel like a ruthless assault where the infant does not empathise with the mother. The aggressive component in primitive love helps the infant to establish a separate external world.

Freud (1917a, pp. 138–139) writes of how the infant may proceed from primitive narcissistic love to object-love as follows:

> At the beginning of the development of the individual all his libido (all his erotic tendencies, all his capacity for love) is tied to himself – that as we say, it cathects his own ego. It is only later that, being attached to the satisfaction of the major vital needs, the libido flows over from the ego on to external objects.

Freud sees the satisfaction of needs, the pleasure, essential for this transition, whereas Winnicott emphasises the aggressive component as necessary for it.

Love is not always ideal, but highly ambivalent, as Freud and Winnicott, for example, have described. Freud (1921c) wrote about love related to sexual love, libido, and Eros. By his concept libido, he meant desire, love, and sexual energy. He stated,

> Libido is an expression taken from the theory of emotions. We call by that name the energy, regarded as a quantitative magnitude ... of those instincts which have to do with all that may be comprised under the word "love". The nucleus of what we mean by love naturally consists (and this is what is commonly called love, and what the poets sing of) in sexual love with sexual union as its aim. (pp. 90–91)

He distinguished between sexual love, tender love, and love for mankind. He also distinguished love between man and woman, parents and children, sibling love, and love for beauty. He stated in the same article that a group is held together by Eros, love, which holds together everything in the world. Freud (1930a) saw the recognition of love as the foundation of civilisation. He has discussed at length the problems of combining love and hatred. Freud (1915c) ascribes ambivalence to the oral-erotic pre-stage of love, where its aim is to devour, to abolish the object. He writes how erotic relationships may be associated with sadistic components, "a quota of plain inclination to aggression" (Freud, 1930a, p. 106).

Winnicott emphasises the coincidence of love and hate (1971, p. 70) in writing, "Health can be looked at in terms of fusion (erotic and destructive drives) and this makes more urgent than ever the examination of the origin of aggression and of destructive fantasy".

Essential in loving and caring relationships is the ability to repair alongside destructive fantasies as Winnicott (1990) states.

Love for the infant may develop in the mother during pregnancy, and even before pregnancy. The mother loves the infant in her mind and her phantasies. Sometimes, however, the mother does not fall in love with her child immediately, or even at all. Falling in love with the infant might take time. Love for the infant naturally makes nurturing the infant and taking responsibility over mothering easier. A mother's love for her baby contains sensual bodily experience. During pregnancy, the heartbeat of the foetus inside the mother, its movements and kicks, strengthen the early contact with the baby and the beginning of love. Breast-feeding, holding the infant in the lap and touching skin-to-skin are sensually pleasurable experiences for both mother and infant. Many women experience orgasmic feelings of pleasure during breast-feeding. Motherhood is also part of the woman's sexual dimension. Mother's love of the third, the baby's father or other companion, is essential for the infant and helps him or her to tolerate separateness and oedipal loneliness.

Love is not always only good and considerate of the other, but often highly ambivalent in adults, too. Love might begin to stifle the other's self, force the other into a fusion or block the other's differentiation. A lover might also deny his or her beloved independent thinking and the right to a different opinion. Two people with a single mind may be the goal of romantic love. Many are familiar with the transitory experience of complete union in orgasm. The pursuit of blissful union belongs to love, but, in its extreme form, the lover might deny the other's separateness.

Maternal love can also be binding to the child and hamper the child's autonomy. It can mean well, but, in fact, be intrusive in the child's life. The mother might meddle with her daughter's relationships or plan the way she should dress, to match her own style, thus failing to respect the daughter's different preferences. In the name of love, the mother might design a life for her child in accordance with her own values and plans, indifferent to the child's separateness. The child does not feel this as love, but as something that negates and suppresses her or his self.

Love can be narcissistically selfish and inconsiderate of the other. The mother might love her child only as a brilliant performer who brings her glory. Besides love, a partner might be sought for value and a boost to one's self-confidence, based on the partner's status, name, or economic well-being. Love always includes so-called good narcissism, the pursuit of one's personal pleasure, but, in bad narcissism, loving the other's well-being is of minor importance and the main thing is the selfish and ruthless furthering of one's own personal pleasure and satisfaction. The mother might use her child as a container for her worries. In the name of love, the mother might use her child as an instrument to express her hatred, like a lightning conductor in the family. Then the other person has no value as such, but is merely a means for obtaining love and boosting one's self-confidence. Good narcissism in loving allows the pursuit of both one's own and the other person's pleasure (Reenkola, 2012).

Love could even have sadistic components, when the aim is to control and dominate the other person, or gain satisfaction from their suffering, or could be masochistic, the aim being submission to the other and suffering. Libido, however, dampens the death drive, as love dampens hatred.

Erotic love contains sexual desire, but sexual desire does not always contain love. Love must be distinguished from the concept of genital primacy.

The conflict between motherhood, work, and sexuality

In my chapter on "Pregnancy, depression and psychoanalysis" (in Reenkola, 2002), I posited that

> Maternal, sexual, and professional desires, including her social life and her friends, are the three main areas of a woman's interest, and it requires skilful balancing if the woman is to avoid feeling that she is sacrificing one of them for the sake of another. These aspirations and their derivatives mix and alternate for the adult woman, and they can conflict with one another. (pp. 21–22)

They might be difficult to combine with each other, which causes ambivalence and conflicts.

Conflict between motherhood and work

Women differ substantially from each other in their attitude to motherhood, and there is much individual variation in their preferences. Not all women want only to stay at home with the infant for ten months on maternity leave. Highly educated women, in particular, who enjoy their work and find it challenging and satisfying, like to get back to work at least part time while still on maternity leave. The work might be creative and interesting and give positive feedback. Advancing in their career and following the developments in their professional field might be important to many, even if they also enjoy nurturing their baby. Caring for a baby and going partially back to work require various compromises. Neither can be a complete commitment, which may cause feelings of guilt in both directions, towards both baby and career.

For some women, returning to work soon after beginning to care for an infant may involve distancing themselves and offer a necessary escape from the infant's binding need and the distress of the symbiotic relationship. At work, things are easier to control and can be put out of mind during the lunch break and after work. Caring for the baby might feel distressingly binding, like submitting completely to the baby's command.

Combining motherhood and sexuality is also a source of conflict for many women. A woman may feel intense sensual pleasure with her infant. Many women have orgasms during breast-feeding. Some are frightened by this, while others are ashamed of it or feel guilt about their pleasure. In Finland, this pleasure can be discussed some-what openly, but in the UK and Australia, for example, it may largely be passed over in silence (personal conversation with Frances Thomson-Salo on 31 May 2013). Can a breast-feeding mother enjoy sex with a man? Many women are not able to combine the two, and sex flags during the time of breast-feeding and infant care. Often, however, pregnancy and childbirth may open up a woman's sexual inhibitions and introduce new dimensions and nuances to her sexual experience. During pregnancy and breast-feeding, sex is, for some, something to avoid, while others might experience it as particularly pleasurable. Many women worry that their body becomes non-erotic and unattractive during pregnancy and breast-feeding.

Why babies?

Why on earth do women still want babies? I have asked this question in women's psychology seminars, and women have invariably been amazed by it. It seems so obvious, and yet, what is obvious about it? Babies tie the woman to the home at least during breast-feeding, threaten equality with men, cost money, etc. Reasons have been sought in biological maternal instinct and social learning, such as roles taught to girls. The wish for motherhood is also believed to arise from cognitive learning: girls are encouraged to play with dolls and at being a mum. Neither learning nor teaching stereotypical sexual roles, however, can completely explain a woman's desire to have a child, and neither does biological maternal instinct. The wish to have a child is also affected by unconscious psychological motives.

The psychologically unique mother–daughter relationship, the experience of similarity and intimacy, helps us understand the deep motives behind the wish for a baby. The experience of similarity and sensual pleasure between a mother and her daughter can, at its best, be blissfully pleasurable. An adult woman wants to re-experience this symbiotic paradise with an infant of her own. At its worst, however, a woman's experience with her mother may have been cold and distant and full of disappointment. Having a baby does not feel so tempting then.

There might be other motives, too, for having a child. The wish to become pregnant or have a baby does not always mean the same as the willingness to take care of a mother's duties. Various narcissistic pursuits are always involved in baby wishes (Reenkola, 2002), and quite naturally so.

- Children can be invested with the continuation of life forever.
- Having a child may include the desire to prove one's femininity or maintain self-confidence.
- A baby may be wanted to regain lost symbiotic contact and satisfy one's own longing for the mother.
- Baby wishes may include the motive of escaping the horror of separateness and independence.
- A baby may be made in the hope of changing or saving the marriage.
- The wish to have a baby might involve the wish to eliminate feelings of depression, emptiness, and loneliness.

Becoming a mother and performing a mother's duties might not always satisfy the mother's unconscious baby wishes. The birth of the baby might be a disappointment to the new mother, particularly when the baby fails to patch up her feminine self-confidence or her marriage. This is apt to cause hatred towards the baby.

Loving and hating the baby

As much as a woman might have wished to have a baby, her feelings towards the foetus may be completely opposite. The foetus growing inside her might feel like a tyrant restricting life. Angry thoughts towards the foetus are quite common in women. Wishes for termination of the pregnancy are common and surface during psychotherapy in particular, even if the pregnancy was wanted. There is reason to worry if the baby does not begin to live in the mother's mind later during the pregnancy. A mother feels hatred and irritation even towards a loved and wanted child, just as even a beloved mother also arouses hatred.

Love and hatred of the child are always intertwined, which creates tension and conflict. Motherhood always causes conflicting feelings: joy and pain, hatred and love, sorrow and happiness, power and weakness, pleasure and displeasure, and the feelings of both power and submission. It is difficult to tolerate conflicting feelings towards significant people. The mother is forced to think of different solutions in order to be able to stand the conflicting feelings towards her child.

A new mother might not always necessarily want her baby, or fall in love it immediately, or even at all. The baby could seem to be a disturbance, someone who turns life upside down, a little dictator. After a traumatically difficult, long, and painful labour, falling in love with the baby might not be easy. A handicap, illness, or even a minor flaw such as birthmarks might come as a shock and weaken the love. The baby is not always the fantasised ideal, but something quite different. It might look like the hated mother-in-law; it might look ugly. It did not turn out to be the flaxen-haired or dark-eyed dream baby. The disappointment, the rage! It is difficult even to speak of it! The desire to become pregnant or have a baby is not at all always the same thing as taking care of a mother's duties and being a parent. The baby turns out to be binding and demands care from morning till night.

Not all mothers share the experience of symbiotic fusion and illusion of oneness with their infant, or feel that the infant is part of their own selves. Yet, this illusion of fusion would be essential to the infant. The infant might seem a stranger to the mother, "a foreign body" or a freak. In the extreme case, the mother might abhor the new-born child as a monster. This is what happened to Mary Shelley's Frankenstein after he had created a monster; he was horrified and ran away immediately, abandoning the creature.

Right from the outset, the mother might also harbour death wishes or murderous thoughts towards her infant alongside her love. These arouse deep guilt and shame in the mother. Women are horrified by their destructive thoughts concerning the infant and fear that they might magically harm the baby. Such thoughts are easily projected inwards and cause severe depression, self-accusations, and ideas of self-destruction.

Phantasy of the murdering mother

In my chapter on "Female aggression" (in Reenkola 2002, p. 83) I wrote,

> Filicide is terrifying and incomprehensible to the extreme. In the unconscious, the phantasy of the murdering mother is quite common. It may appear in at least three variations. The woman may be afraid of being a killer mother herself, a mother who destroys her fertility or her baby. Secondly, the woman's own mother may be the killer in her fantasies. A third version of the phantasy is that the woman's fertility and becoming a mother might magically kill her own mother.

We must remember that death wishes and murderous thoughts, conscious or unconscious, concerning the infant are completely different from actual deeds. They are painful and upsetting, yet universal. The killer mother is an archaic and universal feminine phantasy that often appears triggered by pregnancy or pregnancy wishes. I shall now take a closer look at its three variations.

A woman might fear that she herself is a killer mother. Myths contain different versions of this phantasy. Medea killed her own children. Marianne Leuzinger-Bohleber (2001) has described the unconscious Medea phantasy where the woman thinks she is so evil and her body so magically destructive that she cannot give birth to new life without killing it. She considers this one of the central phantasies for women suffering from psychogenic infertility, but other women have it, too.

In another myth, Jocasta, mother of Oedipus, abandoned him to die in the desert with his feet pierced. Demeter, mother of Kore/ Persephone destroyed the crops of the earth, fertility, and the symbol of a baby. In Finnish lullabies, mothers sing of sending their child to *Tuonela*, the realm of the dead.

A woman might think that she herself magically destroys her fertility. The imagined destruction can happen at any stage: ovulation, the health of the egg cell, conception by sperm, attachment to the wall of the uterus, miscarriage, or damage to the foetus. To my knowledge, psychodynamic factors do not, however, magically cause childlessness.

A pregnant woman is deeply worried about the well-being of the foetus and possible damages to it. Fears concerning deformity of the foetus or genetic deviations such as Down's syndrome, brain damage, tumours, and illnesses haunt almost all expectant mothers. If the baby is born with even a minor flaw or handicap, the mother often experiences intense, tormenting feelings of guilt as well as shame over the fact that the child is not the beautiful, perfect thing of her ideal. Guilt-laden phantasies are common; the woman may worry that she has caused the damage in some magical way.

When a woman chooses to terminate her pregnancy, she might feel relieved but, at the same time, far guiltier than we generally like to think. After making her decision about abortion, it might be difficult for the woman to accept the conflicting feelings it arouses. Even if the abortion can be justified on many acceptable grounds and makes life easier, on an unconscious level it might still cause guilt and the need for self-punishment or redemption. The conflicting factors related to an abortion are the woman's right to decide over her own body, on the one hand, and the rights of the foetus, on the other. Many take the side of the foetus and many others the side of the woman. What makes the matter problematic is the fact that the foetus is at once part of the woman's body and a separate being with its own genes. The rights of the foetus cannot be taken separately from those of the woman, because the foetus is part of the woman. Many women who have had an abortion report still feeling guilty many years later, and guilt might torment them even during later pregnancies. Some say that they count the aborted foetus as part of their number of children and, when the other children are celebrating their birthdays, the mother finds herself thinking of how old her aborted child would have been on that day. It is important that the woman makes room for feelings of guilt over abortion (Reenkola, 2013).

Teresa, a fifty-year-old lower-school teacher was in analysis. She suffered from severe guilt and need for self-punishment for having had an abortion as a teenager after a one-night stand. She blamed herself mercilessly as a child murderer and felt that she had no right to anything good ever since. Finally, at the age of forty, she had a much-wanted child with the help of a donated ovum. Her own ova were no longer fertile enough, and to her, this was punishment for having the abortion in her youth.

A mother's unconscious death wishes or fears concerning her baby may appear in dreams. In the course of psychotherapy, in particular, access to these, often unconscious, wishes may become easier, making it possible to work them through. Leena dreamt that she saved her baby from under a car. The wheel of the car was just driving over the baby's head in the dream, the wish being manifested in the form of fear.

Maija had the following dream towards the end of her pregnancy, a week before giving birth:

> "I was in a big department store, at Stockmann's. Three terrorists attacked me and threatened me with a rifle. There was a naked baby on a landing, safe."

She gave the following associations: the department store alluded to her big, pregnant body; the terrorists represented the three objects of her anger: mother, analyst, and husband. She was also the three terrorists herself. It turned out that she was afraid that her hatred threatened her baby, who was safe in the dream. She feared she was a killer mother who would destroy her baby with her hatred.

The film *A Common Thread* (*Brodeuses*, Faucher, 2004) is a touching description of a young woman's ambivalence in the face of becoming a mother. Teenager Claire becomes pregnant at the age of seventeen in a casual relationship with a married man when the condom breaks. She becomes aware of the pregnancy in the fifth month and does not tell the baby's father. She decides to give the baby away at birth and manages to hide her pregnancy. She destroys the foetus in her mind by thinking of it as a cancerous tumour that will destroy her life force, with her red hair as its symbol. Her shame over the pregnancy is boundless, and she aims to hide and deny the baby's growth inside her. Getting to know an older woman, Madame Mélikian, building a friendship with her, and collaborating in embroidery work help Claire to process her becoming a mother. Mutual friendship is rewarding to both women. Admiration and encouragement concerning her embroidery provided by an older man, fashion guru Christian Lacroix, also helps Claire. She matures psychically and decides to keep the child. Towards the end of her pregnancy, Claire meets a man, Guillaume, to whom she becomes attached and who adores her. The combination of pregnancy and sexual desire between Claire and Guillaume is described tenderly. Guillaume feels passion for the big-bellied Claire, who carries another man's child, and passion for Guillaume is also kindled in Claire—in quite late pregnancy.

Wishes that the infant would die, or plans of murdering the infant might manifest the mother's deep despair and lack of trust in the mother–infant relationship ever growing and producing something good in life. They often manifest fears that one's resources are inadequate for meeting the demands of motherhood. In the background, there are often experiences of not having been a joy, but a disturbance, to one's own mother.

In a woman's unconscious phantasies, her own mother may be a killer mother like Jocasta. At the beginning of the Oedipus myth, mother Jocasta sends her boy to die in the desert, with his feet pierced. The thought or knowledge that one's own mother might wish for one's death is deeply wounding, and mourning it might be difficult. Some mothers, indeed, have told their child about their death wishes.

The unconscious phantasy of a mother's vengeance, causing damage to the infant, sexual pleasure, or fertility, is universal. In Finnish folklore, *Syöjätär*, "Eateress", who comes and snatches the baby away at birth, describes such a phantasy. Easter witches and trolls who come in their envy to harm the neighbours' cows, etc., are presumably of the same kind.

A third version of the unconscious feminine phantasy might be that the woman's fertility could bring destruction on her own mother. The woman may have the phantasy that her becoming a mother could magically kill her mother. It would, therefore, be safest to conceal her fertility and the conceived baby.

Leena, whose story I have described in previous publications (Reenkola, 2008, 2013), hid her pregnancy from her mother for a long time. Haunted by feelings of guilt, she imagined she would sap her mother's life force through her own fertility. Leena thought she might have sapped even my life force, making her see me as old, tired, and exhausted. In expectant women who are in psychotherapy or analysis, phantasies of this kind may be activated in transference as worries about sapping the therapist's life force.

The alternation of hatred and love in motherhood never ends. Loving is the opposite of hating and alleviates the destructiveness of hatred. It is a relief if the mother can allow room in herself even for murderous and death-wishing thoughts towards her infant alongside her love. It is essential to her psychic well-being. Facing conflicting feelings and working them through give the woman psychic flexibility and scope. It can develop into the skill of coping with conflicting and opposite things even in other fields of life, at work, for instance, and in social tasks.

Thought and talk differ from acts. If one is allowed to think angry thoughts in peace from childhood on, or share them verbally with others, they can be bound in words and kept under control. Then they are not so easily projected inwards as depression, or need to be realised by acting out.

Medea's monologue as manifestation of mother's ambivalence

Medea's story is as follows: Medea is an immigrant, a refugee, who rose in popularity thanks to her skills as a sorceress. She left her fatherland, Colchis, when she fell in love with Jason. Medea is described as an active, skilful woman who knows how to use her talents and magic powers to help Jason in his quest for the Golden Fleece. At the beginning of the myth, Medea is an actor and a subject. She commits several murders to clear obstacles from Jason's way. As she flees her fatherland with Jason, Medea murders her brother, who tries to stop them. She lures the daughters of King Pelias into committing patricide in order to allow Jason to obtain the Golden Fleece. Medea and Jason settle down in Corinth and have two sons. Medea helps her husband in every way.

Euripides' play describes the triangle formed by Medea, Jason, and Glauce. Jason betrayed Medea by taking a new wife, the youngest daughter of King Creon, Glauce, in his quest for power. Jason treated Medea shamelessly and unscrupulously. Medea lost everything, her husband, her social status, and her honour when Jason married Glauce. Her sons, too, lost their status. Medea became a humiliated victim. In her shame phantasies, Medea is mocked and ridiculed and turns into a laughable barbarian woman in Jason's eyes. Medea thinks of death as an escape from shame, for both herself and her sons.

Being cast aside in the triangle causes depression and despair in Medea at first. Her combined shame and rage are fatally intensified when Creon tells her that she and her children will be driven into exile. Exile is the last blow and humiliation to Medea. She lets go of her thoughts of death and suicide, as rage and vindictiveness take hold of her entirely. Medea gathers her strength and moves on from womanly timidity, paralysis, and thoughts of suicide to the open fury of vengeance. Her motherly, feminine aspects give way as she puts the tremendous powers of a sorceress to use as her weapons in vengeance. She turns the position of a humiliated, helpless victim upside down, embarking on a grim phallic revenge.

Medea uses her skills as a sorceress to inflict her revenge: she prepares a poisoned gift for her rival, Glauce. She sends her son to take the gift, a poisoned piece of jewellery, to Glauce, who cannot resist wearing it. The poison kills Glauce and her father, who comes to hug his dying daughter. Thus, Medea uses her own children as intermediaries in her murderous vengeance.

Jason had taken everything that was valuable to Medea; she does the same to Jason by destroying what was the most valuable to him, their children. She makes Jason go through her own humiliation, loss, and shame. She wants her husband to suffer, because she has suffered herself. With sadistic cruelty, she sets out to hurt Jason in the most painful way by slaying their children. She calls forth all her skill and power to serve her destructive revenge on Jason. Hatred of Jason has destroyed her earlier love and passion. Motherly love has given way to vindictiveness.

Medea goes through a harrowing struggle in the grip of thoughts of motherly love *vs.* filicide, life drive *vs.* death drive. Medea's monologue before she kills her children poignantly reflects the conflict between vindictiveness and love for her children:

> What misery I've brought on myself!
> It was all for nothing: the pains of labour, years of
> Rearing—
> The worries and the fears of being a mother!
> I had such hopes for you, such hopes:
> That you would care for me when I grew old and,
> When I died, dress me for burial with your own dear hands.
> These dreams were sweet, but have come to nothing.
> Without you, I'll live out my days in pain and grief.
> And you will never again look on your mother
> With those kind and loving eyes.
> You will have gone from me.
>
> To Chorus.
>
> What am I going to do? My heart gives way
> When I see their shining faces. My poor babies.

I can't do it. Forget all the schemes.
I'll take them away with me, away from here.
Why should I hurt them, just to punish him?
When I would suffer twice as much?
I won't do it. I won't think of it again.

But wait, what's going on?
Could I leave here without seeing my enemies punished?
Leave Corinth a laughing stock?
I must steel myself, and do it.
What a coward I am, to let such softness dull my blade.
Children! In, into the house!
Anyone without the stomach for sacrifice: keep well away.
My hand will not weaken now.

No! No! No! Stop this raging of the heart! Let them be,
Monstrous woman, leave their young lives alone!
We could all be happy and safe in Athens . . .
No! No! No! By the furies of Hell,
I'll not abandon them to my enemies and their violation.
It's all done now, anyway; there's no escape.
They must die too. And since they must,
The one who gave them life must be the one to end it.

(Euripides, 2008)

Medea's burning rage and vindictiveness towards Jason ebb and flow, burdened by shame and guilt. Love and tender feelings towards her children make her hesitate time and again. Finally, however, she chooses vengeance, hardening her heart to overcome her shame. She drives herself on to harness her heart. Medea also wants to save her children from worse, the enemy's mockery and ridicule. One motivational thread in the filicide is also her desire to bring the children to safety from the enemy's disdain.

The only power and status left to Medea was her motherhood. All other status she lost when she lost Jason. Medea did not want to murder Jason, because, vindictively and sadistically, she wanted to be there to see his pain. In that she succeeded: Jason felt racking pain and showed it to Medea. "You're not laughing now," Medea says to Jason. Shame is a powerful fuel in Medea's vengeance. She could have gone into exile with her children, to Aegeus, but chose the road of destruction instead.

Euripides' play is searing and gives rise to conflicting feelings. Medea's destructiveness is fearsome, while her earlier pain and despair also arouse sympathy in the reader.

Conflict between shame and honour

There is room in motherhood for shame as well as honour and pride. Shame results when a person reveals their deepest reasons and wishes for longing, but feels unworthy or unlovable as such, unable to fulfil the demands of the ego ideal. The gulf and conflict between demanding ideals and the self lead the person to shame. Ideals are central to the birth of inner shame. A person who acts in accordance with ideals can feel pride and satisfaction. The gap between exorbitant ideals and abysmal feelings of deficiency is soil for shame. This is inner shame, as distinct from outer shame. Outer shame is provoked when a person is shamed, humiliated or ridiculed by others. Disappointments in the pursuit of reciprocity cause shame, as Ikonen and Rechardt (2010) have described. Here, I focus on shame as an inner conflict. Shame is the opposite of pride and honour. Shame is always accompanied by various phantasies of a ridiculing or judging audience. In shame, a person is judged by an inner eye, which weighs how far one has fallen from the ideals.

A woman's ideals: a compass or a corset?

The ideals of motherhood can point the woman in the right direction, as a compass does, or they may be forcefully demanding and strangling, like a corset. The ideal of a good mother guides the woman in caring for her children. If a woman, in her inner evaluation, feels that she falls far short of her maternal ideals, she feels shame.

Ideals are part of the superego. A woman's ideal self contains both feminine and what are generally called masculine pursuits. The feminine core of a woman's ideals is the effort to be like the perfect lost mother of childhood illusions. The ideals of motherhood may guide the woman towards the good aspects of motherhood, putting the child's best interest first. A woman can also strive for perfect, devoted, motherly love through so-called phallic acts: visible academic achievements, success in working life, or celebrity. These are a natural part of the contemporary woman's ideals, although they are some-what misleadingly called phallic or masculine. Success in working life brings the mother satisfaction and is, thus, also beneficial to the child.

The demanding ideals of being a perfect mother and simultane-ously a woman successful in both work and studies naturally exert pressure on the woman. At the same time, they give the woman scope in two directions, which may help her fulfil her potential. No mother of small children can follow the road shown by both compass and corset to the full. Compromises are necessary. The ideals of mother-hood may, in fact, often feel like a strangling corset.

Idealised picture of motherhood

Psychoanalysts often present an idealised picture of the mother that few mothers can ever fulfil in practice. On the other hand, psychoana-lysis has also dismissed and belittled motherhood, like Freud in his writings. The ideal mothers of the motherly myth are praised in poems and songs. They describe how the mother loves, understands, comforts, and alleviates pain. The ideal mother never gets angry with her children or screams at them. More is wanted and expected from the mother than from anyone else in the world, making the disap-pointments all the greater. The myth of the mother has been created to deal with these disappointments and compensate for them. The traditional myth of the mother reflects the kind of mother we were left longing for as children.

Mothers, like other people, have often been narcissistically woun-ded and are unable to act in accordance with the ideals and give primal love and devotion enough to their babies. In my work as a psychotherapist and analyst, in particular, I have met both wounded mothers and children of wounded mothers. The demands of "mater-nal work" might be oppressive for a woman, especially if her demands and helplessness were not tolerated by her own mother. In my chapter "Pregnancy, depression, and psychoanalysis (in Reenkola, 2002, p. 40), I wrote that

> A woman's childhood disappointments are, indeed, profoundly
> reflected in her relationship to her own child. In a woman's psyche,
> growing to be a mother especially tests how, as a child, her own help-
> lessness, desires, and dependency on the mother have been endured

and received. The more feelings of unfulfilment and disappointment the woman has been left with when she was a baby, the more difficult it is for her to be concerned about the distress and demands of her own baby. If longings for maternal care ache in one's own mind, the work of motherhood can feel overwhelming; soothing the baby can arouse intensive envy.

In classic fairy tales, mothers are either idealised or dead. Queen mothers are beautiful, kind, and good, displaying no hatred, vindictiveness, or envy. Destructiveness has been split off from mothers and placed on witches, bad fairies, or bad stepmothers. The child's ambivalence towards the mother has been dissipated by separating love and hatred from each other and placing them in different characters. Only witches try to kill children, never mothers. Princesses love their mothers, while hatred is directed at evil stepmothers and witches. Justice prevails, but not meted out by the woman. Witch women reflect not only the child's fears concerning the mother's hostile and malevolent impulses, but also the child's own hatred towards the mother. In fairy tales, the existence of evil stepmothers depicts the mothers' destructive aspects which have been separated from the good mother. In order to protect the ideal picture of the mother, a child often needs to split off the mother's evil and hateful aspects, as well as her sexuality. The differentiation protects the picture fostered by the child of the mother as a good and protecting being. This is necessary for the child's growth and the development of basic trust. In a child's mind, the mother is almighty and ideally good. Many have remained forever longing for the ideal woman of the mythical mother in their innermost being.

The ideals demanding perfect motherhood may soar out of reach compared with the reality of motherly duty, about which the mother may feel boundlessly bad. If the gap between the two is wide, feelings of shame and insufficiency are provoked in the mother. The shame of a woman striving for the role of the ideal mother is boundless and unreasonable.

Nevertheless, ideals and the motherly myth are necessary as a guideline, as a compass for caring for the infant and taking it into consideration. The direction pointed out by the ideals can be instructive, even if demanding. Caring for, and taking into consideration, a helpless creature acts as a compass. That kind of mother does not leave her baby crying, but tries to alleviate discomfort every time it becomes evident. She does not put the infant's endurance to the test by going away for too long a time. This ideal presupposes—and quite reasonably so—that the mother should not neglect her child psychically or use physical or mental violence towards the child.

However, the bones in the mother's ideal corset are often too hard. According to one ideal, the mother must devote herself completely to the infant and never make a single mistake. She must be perfect, concentrate on her infant with complete self-sacrifice, and give up her own ambitions. The mother of this demanding ideal is always at home and there for the children; she cooks and bakes for her children. She is not allowed to feel hatred towards her children or rage in fury at them. The corset requires that the woman stop dreaming about profession and a career, or self-fulfilment in any other fields in life. Absolute motherhood is submission to the child's ruthless command.

What to do when the child infuriates her boundlessly with defiance, dawdling when they should leave for day care, bullying a smaller sibling, messing with food, or soiling? A mother's own dear children may, quite naturally, raise blind rage in her, which hurts her more deeply than anger at her partner or colleagues. Fortunately, the mother's flashes of anger and bouts of yelling do not harm the child, whereas continuous dismissal and disdain or the use of physical or mental violence do. Getting angry with one's children may, nevertheless, cause profound shame in many.

A corset that is too tight does not allow the mother any pleasure in her sexual relationship, either. Such choking motherhood ideals are often partly unconscious, and the woman might rebel internally against them and wish to stand against their one-sided demands for perfection. They might feel oppressively severe and restrictive of autonomy. The struggle can become quite severe, if the woman feels that the ideals have been imposed on her from the outside.

The child, too, yearns for the illusion of the beloved, wonderful mother. It is needed as a counterweight to the image of the bad and evil mother. In the child's mind, the ideal mother is a counterforce to the witches, evil stepmothers, fairies, and ice queens of the fairy tales, or Snow Hag and Groke of the Moomins' stories.

Shame in motherhood

A woman's value may seem to be determined by the yardstick of motherhood.

A child's disorders, psychic problems, handicaps, physical illness, nausea, or possible accidents hurt the mother and might also cause shame in her. Besides pain and grief, the feeling of failure as a mother leads to mortal shame, even if the woman has been successful in all other fields of life.

A sufficient reason for self-blame might also be that the child does not meet the mother's ideals and wishes—by not being talented, successful, social, beautiful, or intelligent enough. Another reason for shame could be that the child did not turn out the world-famous opera singer, or world champion in sport, or write a brilliant doctoral thesis, but just became an ordinary person.

The bodily changes brought on by pregnancy are not controllable and may, therefore, cause shame as well as gratification. A woman can be proud of her growing belly and want to draw attention to it, but it might also cause shame and the desire to hide and cover her belly. It is the sign of a sexual relationship, of sin, etc. In labour, the woman is unable to control her own body; labour begins in its own good time. The uterus contracts, the waters break and flow, and excrement and urine may escape from the woman in the middle of labour. During the period of breast-feeding, rising milk stains the blouse. This messiness might embarrass a woman, rather as childhood incontinence did.

Women often try to hide the problems of motherhood, because they easily feel inferior when falling short of the ideal mythical mother. They might dismiss any problems with breast-feeding. Today, the demands and problems of motherhood are increasingly discussed in the media and on the Internet, which helps in facing the shame. Women are nowadays encouraged in the media to deal with the problems of motherhood instead of keeping silent about them. The ideals of the motherhood myth are being dismantled with an encouraging vigour. Peer groups have been founded where women can deal with these problems. Many women and their children benefit from this development. Yet, notwithstanding, postpartum depression is still considered shameful, and the obstacles to seeking therapy often seem insuperable.

Fertility is associated with shameful things, but childlessness, too, is shameful and a thing to hide. Miscarriages and abortions can be so hurtful and shameful that the woman keeps silent about them and hides them. Fertility treatments help many childless couples, but they may also cause shame over the fact that the couple did not manage to conceive a child by their own means.

There is room for shame but also pride in the vulnerable area of motherhood. A woman feels proud giving birth to her baby, if the delivery goes without severe complications. She could give birth unashamed in the middle of the railway station, even if she is otherwise modest. Giving life can be such a tremendous thing.

The children's growth and progress, and their successes, are causes of joy and pride for the mother. Her grief is without bounds if the child's life does not run smoothly. Children are, after all, part of the mother's self, even when they grow up.

Shaming is sometimes considered an effective method of education. Mothers often use mockery and embarrassment without being aware of doing so. A mother might tell her relatives or friends funny stories about the child even when the child is within hearing, or make outspoken comments on how the child looks, without realising how humiliating this is to the child. Mockery and embarrassment are specifically directed at the child's helplessness and incompetence. "A big girl like you, you should be able to do it by now," slips from many. Being called a wet blanket ridicules the crying child.

Shame can, of course, also be constructive. Mild shame curbs the realisation of desires and helps control them. Shame drives people away from self-centredness to pay attention to others, dampens uncritical self-contentedness and feelings of superiority and humbles people to consider their personal failures, mistakes, and imperfection. Shame can prevent the mother from making her child cry, or hitting her child. A shameless person does not feel guilt about his or her deed, or concern for others. Mild shame is a prerequisite of reciprocity in human relationships, but pathological shame paralyses and brings great pain.

A narcissistically damaged mother is not usually able to feel shame. She may have been hurt and humiliated so badly that she has broken all contact with her wounds and isolated them behind multiple walls. She dares not feel shame, because it might be too crushing. The mother will then place the shame outside her, or shame and humiliate her children unconsciously by transferring her own psychic wounds to them.

If the spouse shames and humiliates the woman as a mother, she might be provoked by shame and rage to seek revenge blindly, even violently, and use her children as intermediaries. This can happen in difficult divorces. It was also what Medea did in the myth when Jason had deprived her of all value and status. Shame and humiliation drove her to revenge by using her children as the instrument. She tried to restore her pride as a woman by transforming from a humiliated victim to a powerful avenger and, thereby, also restore her sense of honour.

How does a woman deal with her shame, which goes against her ideals and which she cannot be proud of?

Some women hide their problems or retreat from situations where they would be revealed. Others are paralysed by shame and lose their initiative. Yet others begin to belittle the thing they are ashamed of, stripping it of meaning and value. They might dismiss the value of motherhood in public, or play down the importance of the mother to an infant. Is it shameful today to be a motherly woman and to enjoy taking care of small children?

Women might try to turn shame into shamelessness and be proud of that. Vulnerability and timidity must be converted into toughness and touted in public. A mother might boast about how her small children can take care of their own meals and that they can easily be left at home alone while the mother is away at work. Some might brag about what negligent, bad mothers they are. Phallic self-sufficiency is an ideal to many, even in motherhood. The shamed woman might refuse to be paralysed and, instead, gather her strength to act as the one who shames.

The contents of women's ideals have changed, though shame has not disappeared. The focus has shifted from the ideals of motherhood to ideals that emphasise success in working life outside the home, building a career, rising to a leading position at work or in politics, making money, travelling on business, becoming famous. Hardness and the use of ruthless tactics to get ahead have become women's ideals, too. The mother who stays at home to take care of her children is not the ideal today. Today, the ideal may be a woman in an executive position.

A woman's ideals have, indeed, changed, and aggression, the expression of hatred and violence to protect both oneself and one's children, is more acceptable than before. Ideals may include violent acts and revenge.

On the other hand, ideals no longer demand complete silence concerning the problems and quandaries of motherhood. They and mothers' ambivalence can be talked and written about more widely and more openly. The mother's ideal corset has slackened a little.

To sum up

Thought and talk are different from acts. If angry thoughts and feelings of hate have been contained and tolerated since childhood by her significant people without retaliation, the woman will be able to harness them in words. Aggressions and death wishes do not then turn inward and develop into depression so easily, or need be acted out. If a girl is treated with concern by her mother and allowed to be separate, helpless and insufficient, yet loved as she is, shame will not have a fertile ground to grow in. The tolerance of ambivalence and the ability to fuse love and hate together is vital even to mothers. Instead of violent acts, revenge, or self-destruction, the mother will then have more capacity for concern and compassion towards her children's separateness, desires and feelings of love and hate.

Note

1.   Translated by Kaisa Sivenius.

References

Alizade, M. (1999). *Feminine Sensuality*. London: Karnac.

Alizade, M. (2006). The non-maternal psychic space. In: M. Alizade (Ed.), *Motherhood in the Twenty-first Century*. London: Karnac.

Balint, M. (1952). *Primary Love and Psycho-Analytic Technique*. London: Hogarth.

Covington, C., & Wharton, B. (2003). *Sabina Spielrein: Forgotten Pioneer of Psychoanalysis*. New York: Brunner-Routledge.

Cronenberg, D. (2011). *A Dangerous Method* (film).

Euripides (2008). *Medea*, R. Robertson (Trans.). New York: Free Press.

Faucher, E. (2004). *A Common Thread* (*Brodeuses*) (film).

Freud, S. (1905d). *Three Essays on the Theory of Sexuality*. S. E., 7: 125–245. London: Hogarth.

Freud, S. (1915a). Instincts and their vicissitudes. S. E., 14: 133–138. London: Hogarth.

Freud, S. (1915c). Instincts and their vicissitudes. S. E., 14: 111–140. London: Hogarth.

Freud, S. (1917a). A difficulty in the path of psycho-analysis. *S. E.*, *17*: 135–144. London: Hogarth.

Freud, S. (1920g). *Beyond the Pleasure Principle*. *S. E.*, *18*: 7–64. London: Hogarth.

Freud, S. (1921c). *Group Psychology and the Analysis of the Ego*. *S. E.*, *18*: 67–143. London: Hogarth.

Freud, S. (1930a). *Civilization and its Discontents*. *S. E.*, *21*: 59–145. London: Hogarth.

Green, A. (1999). *The Work of the Negative*. London: Free Association Books.

Ikonen, P. & Rechardt, E. (2010). *Thanatos, Shame, and other Essays*, K. Sivenius & L. Siilasvuo (Trans.). London: Karnac.

Laplanche, J., & Pontalis, J.-B. (1973). *The Language of Psycho-analysis*. London: Karnac.

Leuzinger-Bohleber, M. (2001). The "Medea fantasy": an unconscious determinant of psychogenic sterility. *International Journal of Psycho-analysis, 82*: 323–345.

Olshansky, D. (Ed.) (n.d.). Gallery of Russian thinkers. Sabina Spielrein. Available at: www.isfp.co.uk.

Reenkola, E. (2002). *The Veiled Female Core*. New York: Other Press.

Reenkola, E. (2004). Sister fantasy in Edith Södergran's poems "Fantastique". *Scandinavian Psychoanalytic Review, 27*: 12–19.

Reenkola, E. (2008). *Nainen ja viha* [Female Aggression]. Helsinki: Minerva.

Reenkola, E. (2012). *Äidin valta ja voima* [Maternal Power and Strength]. Helsinki: Minerva.

Reenkola, E. (2013). Vicissitudes of female revenge. In: I. Moeslein-Teising & F. Thomson- Salo (Eds.), *The Female Body: Inside and Outside* (pp. 201–220). London: Karnac.

Roos, E. (2008). Some thoughts on happy and unhappy love. *Scandinavian Psychoanalytic Review, 31*(2): 77–85.

Shakespeare, W. (2011). *Romeo and Juliet*. London: Harper Press.

Spielrein, S. (1995). Destruction as cause of becoming. *Psychoanalysis and Contemporary Thought, 18*: 85–118.

Winnicott, D. W. (1971). *Playing and Reality*. London: Tavistock.

Winnicott, D. W. (1984). *Deprivation and Delinquency*. London: Tavistock.

Winnicott, D. W. (1990). Psychoanalysis and the sense of guilt. In: *The Maturational Processes and the Facilitating Environment* (pp. 16–28). London: Karnac.

CHAPTER FIVE

Female destructiveness in fairy tales and myths

Anneli Larmo

Introduction

We read more and more often in newspapers of violent acts performed by girls and women. One such report was published in *Helsingin Sanomat* in September 2011. It stated that girls between twelve and eighteen years old accepted beating and were not ashamed to express violence. On the other hand, the same article declared that, when interviewed, the same girls said that one should not hit other people and that conflicts ought to be resolved by talking. In October 2011, the newspaper reported that teenage girls physically attacked their peers in Espoo and, in April, 2012 another newspaper, *Hufvudstadsbladet*, wrote, "The woman who killed her two children mitigated her crime by saying that she wanted to punish her husband for having left her and the children for another woman". What do such news stories tell us about girls and young women today? What is our relationship to girls' and women's violence today? Do we judge it more severely than boys' violent behaviour? What about the cultural norms: are they different for boys and girls? Finally, how do the unconscious wishes, fears, and fantasies about woman/mother affect our relationship to girls' and women's violence?

Is our society still patriarchal? Do we condemn women's or girls' violence but accept violent behaviour in boys? According to some research findings (Brown et al., 2007), more court cases for violence were brought against girls for less severe offences than against boys and, at the same time, violence performed on girls was devalued. We might draw a conclusion from the result that the girls are expected to be more well behaved and good than boys. Girls should not lift their hand against the other, but the violence towards them is approved. Goodkind and colleagues (2009) equally declare that girls' violence actually has not increased but that they are charged on lesser grounds. On the other hand, the girls that have been charged with violent acts have themselves been more often maltreated emotionally, physically, or sexually in their childhood or youth, and they frequently have an attachment trauma (Heide & Solomon, 2009).

Violence as such is not badness or evilness, but can be used to express bad or evil intentions. What, then, is badness? To be bad, one has to consciously and intentionally want to harm the other. In this chapter, I try to depict women's badness and goodness from the viewpoint of the dualistic drive theory. Freud mentions the dualistic drive theory for the first time in *The Ego and the Id* (1923b) and he develops it for the rest of his life. The last mention is in "Analysis terminable and interminable" (1937c). Freud has taken the idea from the ancient philosopher Empedocles, who depicts human life as a constant battle between two opposing forces, destruction and love. In this battle, either love or destruction is first winning and then defeated, to win again in the ongoing battle. The destructive drive that Freud depicts is later called Thanatos, the death drive. The life drive, which Freud called Eros, arouses tensions as it joins people and things together and looks for satisfaction. The death drive, or the destructive drive, is in a dialectic relationship to this. The death drive is in opposition to the life drive. It aims at peace and quiet and ridding of disturbing stimuli (Freud, 1937c, Ikonen & Rechardt, 2004). These two drives, or their dialectic relationship, keep the pulsation of life going. To be exact, neither drive is good or bad, but they create together a tension, which goes on through the life cycle.

The destructive death drive, Thanatos

The human being strives towards equilibrium, like all living matter. All living systems try to restore their equilibrium whenever it is threatened. Likewise, the death drive restores the harmony in humans whenever the life drive and its tension threatens to disrupt it. We cannot see the working of the drives directly. They are expressed as derivatives and seen in the human's striving towards peace of mind and body whenever that is disturbed. Thus, for instance, in situations where a person's identity or existence is threatened, and he/she feels helpless and his/her psychological resources are inadequate to restore the equilibrium, his/her only way to restore inner peace might be the violent destruction of either one's self or the other.

After Sigmund Freud, Melanie Klein (1946) in particular discusses the death drive (Ogden, 1990). She sees the death drive working in the so-called paranoid–schizoid position. In that position, Klein postulates that the child's original envy and greed towards the mother's breast stimulates in the infant a wish to destroy the breast in order to avoid the painful and distressing feelings aroused by it. We can imagine that the infant is in this kind of state of mind when, for instance, it has waited too long to be fed. In this position the child does not experience itself as a whole subject or the other as a whole object, good and bad, but either good or bad, depending on whether its needs are satisfied or not. To be able to maintain a good image of oneself or the other, the child splits the good and the bad object and self-representation from each other. Then, the good and bad representations are kept apart in an attempt to protect the good from the bad. That results in the good not being able to alleviate the effect of the bad representations. After the split is effective, one can project the bad or the good representations on the other. It saves one from experiencing bad impulses or ideas, or saves the good from one's own badness. The bad does not now attack from within, but one is threatened from the outside. That makes the outer world dangerous and menacing and, to cope with that, one has to try to control it. In the paranoid–schizoid position, control is facilitated by the fantasy of both omnipotence and the ability to repair by magic the destruction caused. Therefore, the person does not feel responsible for his/her deeds and does not suffer from guilt feelings. The development and growth in relation to another person gradually takes the child towards a whole self and object representation and the so-called depressive position. Then the person feels responsibility for what he/she has done to the other. It arouses feelings of guilt and the person wants to make up for the evil he/she has done. The badness makes him/her feel sad and responsible for that part of his /her personality also. When both positions are developed, they alternate through the whole life cycle, as do the life and the death drives (Ogden, 1990). Problems arise if either one has supremacy over the other.

I wish to discuss the meaning of destructive drives, not only in badness, but also in goodness. Even the death drive strives from the point of view of the subject towards satisfaction, when it returns the human being to a state of peace (Ikonen & Rechardt, 2004). To achieve that, the destruction of the other is sometimes necessary and, thus, the death drive can serve an evil purpose at the same time.

What is the meaning of violence?

What does violence serve? What is the psychological meaning of it? How are violence, aggression, and badness related to each other? When Freud created his dualistic drive theory with the life and the death drive, he abandoned the former theory of the ego drives and the sexual drive. This change was not received with approval only. If one reads Freud thoroughly and is acquainted with writings of Ikonen and Rechardt (2004), who argue that the death drive is a drive that strives for peace and is in opposition to Eros, the life drive, which seeks satisfaction from joining objects and ideas to each other, but also creates tension and threatens the equilibrium of the organism and arouses feelings of unpleasure, one is compelled to regard the death drive also as a drive that is not synonymous with aggression. To fulfil its purpose, peace, the death drive might have to use destructive or aggressive means, which does not necessarily mean that the death drive is a destructive drive and the life drive is not. Sometimes Eros, too, might use destructive means to reach its goal, as in erotic sadism (Freud, 1923b).

We connect a certain amount of psychic energy to the aggressive affect. It can be regarded as the power the ego needs to fulfil its purposes. The result may be good or bad, depending on how this power is used. If I use my aggressive energy to make myself write this chapter, we might think that it results in something positive and productive. If, on the other hand, I use my aggression to destroy an article written by somebody else because of envy, the result is destructive. Thus, violence is just one way of using or discharging aggressive energy.

When the other person becomes bad or threatening in our minds, we do not question our actions, but feel justified in taking it. When feelings of envy or jealousy occupy our minds, we wish to destroy the one that causes us the unpleasant feelings. Envy makes us feel that the other, merely by existing, threatens our being. So, is an envious person bad? Our superego keeps watch over what is right and what is wrong, but as the superego is also a developmental acquisition, one may lose its function depending on whether one is in the paranoid–schizoid or the depressive position. Violence might express the badness of a person, but we might also regard it as the ultimate method of survival in situations of extreme helplessness. Perelberg (1999), in trying to understand the meaning of violence, regards it as a way of regulating identity in circumstances where no better means are available. These are situations in which the person's total being is threatened by intolerable feeling states such as intensive shame or helplessness. Then the violence against oneself or the other restores the experience of integrity and control. Here, we can see the death drive trying to restore peace and equilibrium to the mind. The violence is directed towards oneself or the other, depending on whether the threat is experienced as coming from inside or from outside. In this way, violence can be used to regulate affects when self-reflection or mentalisation is lacking. If such behaviour is structuralised, it becomes a part of the personality, and becomes a way of relating to other people without the need for a trigger (Fonagy et al., 1992).

The badness of women in fairy tales

I will now try to shed light on the badness of women with the help of two fairy tales by the brothers Grimm: *Little Snow-White* and *The Sleeping Beauty*. Traditionally, we look at these fairy tales from the point of view of the heroine, who is a young, beautiful, and good maiden in both. Beauty and goodness are usually connected to each other. The heroine is the object of identification to the young reader, usually a girl. Behind this picture of goodness stands the picture of the idealised childhood mother, good and beautiful. Yet, as we know, the early mother is not only good and beautiful. She is also, from the child's perspective, dangerous and bad in her omnipotence and when she does not satisfy the child's need or when the child is afraid of losing her love. This early mother figure is at the heart of both the girl's and the boy's identification with the omnipotent, early mother.

Little Snow-White

The Grimms' fairy tale *Little Snow-White* starts by describing a queen wishing for a child as red as blood, as white as snow, and as black as ebony. She then gives birth to a beautiful girl child, Snow-White, but dies, and, after a year has passed, the king takes another queen who is beautiful but vain.

The image of the woman is, from the very beginning, divided into two. The original mother queen and her daughter are totally good and the stepmother queen is totally bad. Snow-White's beauty emphasises her goodness, while envy and vanity destroy the beauty of the step-mother. In the small child's mind, the good and bad object and self - representations are still separated from each other and the self is easily experienced as either good or bad. Also, an adult may return to this paranoid–schizoid way of experiencing life, particularly if the mind is filled with envy or jealousy. The fairy tale's way of making the characters either good or bad helps the child to deal with the opposite feelings in his/her own mind (Klein, 1946).

The queen is shown as beautiful, but her beauty is spoilt by her envy and arrogance, which also make her vulnerable. Her pride does not allow that anybody else in the kingdom would be more beautiful than she. Her magic mirror verifies repeatedly that she is still the most beautiful. One day, however, when she asks the looking-glass: "Mirror, mirror, on the wall, who in this land is the fairest of all?", the mirror unexpectedly does not give the usual reply, but answers, "Thou art fairer than all who are here, Lady Queen. But more beautiful still is Snow-white, as I ween". The queen's world crashes about her when she hears the answer. The story then continues and tells us how the queen's unbearable envy demands that Snow-White has to be destroyed. Only then will the queen's peace of mind be restored. She decides to have Snow-White killed but her plan does not succeed as her gamekeeper's heart is too soft and he leaves Snow-White in the woods instead of murdering her, as he had been instructed. When the queen hears that Snow-White is still alive she decides to do something about it herself, and is able to trick Snow-White into biting a poisoned apple. That bite gets stuck in Snow-White's throat and, unable to breathe, she dies. When the dwarfs, with whom she is living in the woods, return home from the mines, they find Snow-White dead, but as she is so beautiful they do not have the heart to bury her, but instead make a coffin of glass and put her in it. One day, a prince, while hunting in the woods, rides past Snow-White's coffin, and when he sees the beautiful Snow-White lying in her glass casket he falls in love with her, and begs the dwarfs to let him take the casket to his castle, where he would make her his wife. But the road is winding and bumpy, and the casket is bouncing about on the horse's back and suddenly the apple is dislodged, and Snow-White is able to breathe again. Snow-White is then married to the prince and the bad queen is punished accordingly. In Walt Disney's film of the story, she falls into a ravine and only a pillar of smoke is left of her. In the tales of the Grimm brothers, the queen has to dance at Snow-White's wedding in flaming shoes until she falls dead on the floor.

Little Snow-White is usually thought of as depicting a young girl's development. In that case, her death would stand for latency, from which she awakens into adolescence, but what is the meaning of the queen, except to be an evil opposition to Snow-White's goodness? Could she have a meaning of her own? What might she represent? We might think that the evil stepmother or queen is the mother image the girl has to separate from in adolescence and whom she has to kill figuratively. She is the equivalent of the oedipal mother, with whom the girl is rivalrous, and whose revenge she might, therefore, be afraid of. The fairy tale tells us about a young developing girl's world and life as she fantasises it. The girl has to murder the oedipal mother image to be able to take possession of her own sexual body. In *Little Snow-White*, the badness of the queen might give the girl the right to do it. Yet, the mother is also an important object of identification for the girl. Could the evil queen be, in some way, a positive object of identification? Yes, she could. For the child, the bad mother is the one who is not at the child's command. She is the mother who has her own life outside the mother—child relationship. It is important for the girl to create space for her own needs and not only pander to the needs of the other. That becomes possible after identification with the more "selfish" mother.

On the other hand, the bad mother and the stepmother represent those parts of the mother into which the girl can project her rivalry and aggression. Thus, the evil stepmother is also important as a receiver and container of the girl's aggressive feelings. It seems to be more difficult for the girl than for the boy to face and express angry feelings in a society where the girl is still expected to be sweet and good and in better control of her feelings than the boy. On the surface, the fairy tale gives preference to a woman who is good and beautiful, who serves others, and has no needs of her own. Snow-White serves the dwarfs and is passively driven, while apparently dead, to be married to the prince passing by. In the evil queen, the tale may also picture other parts of the girl or woman unconsciously. Thus, we can enjoy identifying with the bad queen's selfishness and badness without feeling guilt.

The Sleeping Beauty

In the Grimm brothers' fairy tale, *The Sleeping Beauty* (1999, pp. 118–123), the plot is like the one in *Little Snow-White*. Here, too, there is a beautiful and innocent young girl, who becomes the victim of an older woman's vengeance. The details are different in the two fairy tales. *The Sleeping Beauty* starts with a description of the princess's birth. After years of longing for a child, the king and the queen have finally got one. The king, therefore, wants to celebrate her christening magnificently. He wants to invite all the wise women in the kingdom to the christening in order that the child will receive presents from them such as beauty, virtue, wisdom, and so on. The problem is that the king wants to use his golden plates in the celebration and there are only twelve of them, whereas the number of the wise women is thirteen. Thus, one of the wise women has to be left out because of the king's vanity. The fairy tale does not differentiate between the wise women in the beginning; the one left out is not worse or more evil than the others. The Disney version of this fairy tale is different. That depicts three good fairies and one evil one, which is not the case in the Grimms' story. The thirteenth wise woman becomes bad because she is offended at being left out and decides to exact revenge. Therefore, she suddenly appears at the christening of the princess and gives her a present, which is a prophecy that the princess, on her fifteenth birthday, will be pricked by the spindle of a spinning wheel and fall down dead. The twelfth wise woman has not given her gift yet; she cannot, however, reverse the prophecy, but only change it to another in which the princess will not die, but fall into sleep for

100 years. The king, in order to prevent the realisation of the predic-
tion, orders that every spinning wheel in his kingdom be destroyed.
But, in one of the towers in the royal castle is a locked room, and to
that room the princess wanders on her fifteenth birthday, and she
finds in the room three women spinning and wishes to try herself.
When she is given the shuttle, she pricks her finger and falls asleep
as predicted, and so does the whole court with her. When 100 years
have passed, a prince hears about a castle totally covered by roses,
where it is said a princess lies asleep. Many young men have tried to
get to the princess but failed. This prince now succeeds in making
his way into the castle, and finds there the most beautiful sleeping
princess. She is so beautiful that he cannot prevent himself from
kissing her, and when he does, she wakes up, and with her the rest
of the court.

   This tale, like that of *Little Snow-White* is also a story of a young
girl's development from latency to adolescence and young adulthood.
After waking up, the princess is ready to marry the prince and they
live happily ever after, but what about the evil woman? In *The Sleeping
Beauty*, the thirteenth wise woman has a more meaningful role than
the wicked queen in *Little Snow-White*. I think that she represents time,
the transience of life, and confronts us with reality, the limited span of
life, and the end of the childhood paradise. She might also represent
the omnipotent early mother who governs both life and death in our
unconscious.

Death and the mother

Freud (1913f) describes in "The theme of the three caskets" how death
is depicted in literature. He says that death is often in the shape of a
young and beautiful woman. That reminds us of the mother figure of
our early childhood: young, beautiful, and good. In the arms of such
a woman we would like to die in old age. At the same time, the fact
that death is depicted as a young woman expresses our wish to deny
it, which we do, like the king in *The Sleeping Beauty*. That is why the
thirteenth wise woman is not invited. She is death, the unwelcome
guest of the celebration. That gives the fairy tale a sombre undertone;
a shadow is thrown on the story, which, on the surface, is a tale of the
development of a young girl and life that goes on.

The girl/the woman can project on to the bad stepmother the evil parts, which do not belong to the idealised picture of herself or the idealised mother. What would the fairy tales *Little Snow-White* or *The Sleeping Beauty* be like without the bad queen or the revengeful wise woman? Their appearance gives the stories a tension similar to that between the death and the life drives envisaged by Freud. The alternation of these drives gives life its tension and feeling of vitality and the fairy tales more depth.

Why do we shun of the idea of women's envy, selfishness, aggression, or violence? What frightens us? Does it perhaps remind us of the early mother's dreadful omnipotence from the child's view point and, thus, threaten to destroy the idealised picture of the all-good mother? Do we have to deny the woman's own needs and her aggressive feelings in order to hold on to the picture of a totally good mother and a fantasy of man's immortality.

Where is the woman's aggression?

The oedipal development of a girl is more complicated than that of a boy, because she has to change the object of her passion. At first, the object is the mother, and then the father usually becomes the object of her love. The girl identifies at first with the early mother whom she believes to be omnipotent and only hers, even if that mother sometimes also is frustrating. The oedipal mother differs from the idealised mother of early infancy. Now, she becomes a mother with needs of her own and a special relationship to the father. In the oedipal phase, the girl turns towards the father in her own expectations of love. The father now becomes both her object of identification and her passion. On the other hand, the girl also identifies with the mother, who loves the father and whom father loves. Because the girl also loves the mother, she becomes scared about losing mother's love, if she wants to have the father for herself. If, on the other hand, she idealises the father and devalues the mother and femininity as an object of identification, the girl's femininity is endangered. In an ordinary oedipal development, the girl identifies also with her father and acquires a positive capacity to use aggressive energy and initiative, and is then able to turn towards her mother to identify with her creative womanhood. She is like Persephone in the ancient myth. Persephone is the queen of the underworld, who lives one half of the year as the spouse of Hades in the kingdom of death and the other half with her mother, the nature goddess, Demeter, on the earth. Some psychoanalysts think that the Persephone myth, or Chore myth, as it is also called, depicts the girl's oedipal development better than the tragedy *Oedipus Rex*.

When all goes well, the girl becomes a woman with her own needs and her own direction in life and, at the same time, a creative woman and mother. The denial of the aggressive parts or their insufficient integration might lead to passivity, lack of initiative, and masochistic self-expression in girls and women. Then the aggression turns inwards towards oneself, or is expressed indirectly. Does the woman's depression or masochism begin here? Sometimes, one sees family violence against women where the woman unconsciously imagines that the cruelty towards her causes suffering in the perpetrator, and she is unable to stop the violence as it serves, unconsciously, her own inhibited aggression towards the other. This, again, could depend on the woman's difficulty in expressing aggression directly. We may understand this from a cultural point of view. In our western culture, women are often ashamed of their aggressive feelings and of openly expressing them, therefore they tend to use social violence to express aggression: expelling someone from a group, speaking ill of others behind their backs, bantering, or withdrawing into martyrdom. The woman's revenge might also be indirect. When aggressive feelings, envy, deep hurt, or hate directs our behaviour and we have to get rid of these feelings because they are unbearable, then we see the death drive in action.

Medea

In another classical play, *Medea* (Euripides, 1963), the heroine kills her children to revenge herself on her husband, who has abandoned her for another woman. The father of her two sons, Jason, Medea's husband, cannot understand her deed. He thinks that Medea should have accepted her fate, even if he could give no guarantees as to the life and safety of Medea and her sons in the future. We might have accepted it had Jason killed his sons on the grounds that they would threaten his future children's succession to the throne. We might even think that he had no choice, but do we understand what Medea did or are we terrified?

In a situation of this kind, the man would be more likely to have killed the person who had offended him. According to that line of thought, Medea should have killed her deceitful husband, Jason, instead of her sons. We are not horrified by the knowledge that Jason, a hero of the Trojan War, has killed maybe hundreds of enemy soldiers. We think that killing in war is more honourable because it has an identifiable cause, such as defending one's country. Medea is not totally without guilt either. She has destroyed her father and brothers, who opposed her marriage to Jason. She has killed for passion and love. Is that not as good a reason for killing as is the love of one's nation? Is it because of Medea's unacceptable reason for killing that we regard her as a violent person who would do such an awful thing as to kill her children? The tale possibly arises in our suppressed unconscious fantasies about the almighty mother, who rules over both birth and death and, as such, threatens our existence.

Mother Holle

The Grimms' tale *Mother Holle* reminds me of the Persephone myth and could depict the oedipal development in the girl of the woman's fertility. It also depicts the change of seasons and the fertility cycle of the earth.

The fairy tale begins:

> There was once a widow who had two daughters—one of whom was pretty and industrious, whilst the other was ugly and idle. But she was much fonder of the ugly and idle one, because she was her own daughter; and the other, who was a stepdaughter, was obliged to do all the work, and be the 'Cinderella' of the house. Every day the poor girl had to sit by the well, in the highway, and spin and spin till her fingers bled.

The beautiful daughter then accidentally drops the shuttle in the well when she washes the blood off it. The blood on the shuttle could also refer to the girl's adolescence and the beginning of menstruation. The girl starts to weep and goes to the stepmother to tell her about the mishap and is told to fetch the shuttle from the well. The poor girl returns to the well and jumps in; she becomes unconscious in the fall and wakes up in a beautiful meadow. She then starts to walk and comes to a baker's oven full of bread. The bread calls, "Oh, take me out! Take me out! Or I shall burn; I have been baked a long time!"

The girl does as she is told and takes one loaf after the other out of the oven until it is empty. Then she comes to an apple tree full of fruit: The tree cries to her, "Oh, shake me! Shake me! We apples are all ripe!" And the girl shakes the tree until all the apples are down. At last she comes to a small cottage and meets an old woman there. The woman looks frightening and the girl is about to turn away when the old woman asks her, "What are you afraid of, dear child? Stay with me; if you will do all the work in the house properly, you shall be the better for it. Only you must take care to make my bed well, and to shake it thoroughly till the feathers fly—for then there is snow on the earth. I am Mother Holle." The girl stays and serves Mother Holle well. Gradually, she starts longing to go back home on earth, even if her life is much better with Mother Holle. Mother Holle understands her wish and takes her to a door. When the girl passes through "the doorway, a heavy shower of golden rain fell, and the gold clung to her, so that she was completely covered over with it". She is given the gold because she has been industrious and she also gets back her lost shuttle. When she walks into the yard of her home, the cock sees her and cries, "Cock-a-doodle-doo! Your golden girl's come back to you." The stepmother and stepsister want to know what has happened, and when the girl tells her story the mother decides that her own ugly and idle daughter, too, must have the same good fortune as the stepdaughter. She sends her daughter to spin at the well, but, because she is idle, she does not want to spin, so simply drops the shuttle into the well and then jumps after it. She, too, comes to the meadow and sees the oven full of bread and the tree full of apples, but she refuses to help because that would make her dirty. She is not only lazy, but also contemptuous. At last she comes to Mother Holle's house and she hires herself to Mother Holle. There, too, she is lazy and does not fluff the old woman's pillows and cover properly and finally Mother Holle gives her notice, and the girl is more than happy to leave. She then goes through the doorway and expects gold to rain over her, but instead a kettleful of pitch is emptied on her. "That is the reward for your service", said Mother Holle, and shut the door. The tale ends with the following words: "But the pitch clung fast to her, and could not be got off as long as she lived".

How could we interpret this fairy tale? The story seems to be connected with harvest time and, through that, with the different seasons and fertility. What else do we see? We see the woman once again split into a totally good and a totally bad part. There is the good and indus-trious daughter, and the bad and idle daughter, the totally bad step-mother and the good and just Mother Holle. Neither of the daughters has a name; they are called the good and beautiful daughter and the ugly and idle daughter. That gives us the impression of one daughter with opposite qualities. The fact that the mother loves the ugly and idle daughter, who is good in her eyes, and that she hates the good daughter, furthers our fantasy of one whole daughter with opposing features. Depending on who is looking at her or how she is looked at, she seems either good or bad. Despite all her beauty and goodness, the mother cannot love her and see her goodness, which Mother Holle does and covers her with gold. Or we might think that the good and beautiful daughter envies the other one, whom she believes the mother is more fond of and, therefore, the sister seems bad and ugly, and the mother feels like a stepmother because of the girl's fantasy that the mother loves the sister more. The envy takes the child into the paranoid–schizoid way of experiencing. In that position, the envy is projected on the other, who then becomes frightening and evil.

In the fairy tale, the girl's shuttle falls into the well, and the girl then courageously enters the underworld. The underworld, or the world of the dead, could stand for the human unconscious. In this subterranean world, goodness is rewarded. Thus, the girl can experi-ence satisfaction. We could also suppose that in this world the girl's longing for love is met. She might think, "Here I am valued and rewarded with gold." On the other hand, Mother Holle could also represent the oedipal father, who sets limits and separates the child from the pre-oedipal mother, or to whom the oedipal girl could turn, in her disappointment with the mother. The same could be said of Hades, which separates Persephone from her mother, Demeter, in the myth.

The girl listening to the fairy tale can identify with Mother Holle as the oedipal father and derive from that identification support for her courage and actions. The girl cannot, however, stay in the under-world if she wants to become a woman. The reality has to be faced on the earth. The girl longs to return to home. The longing contains the image of a good enough mother. We could also say that the under-world is not satisfactory in the long run with its omnipotent way of experiencing things. The girl's development demands a move towards the depressive position, which leaves room for longing and sadness in the girl's mind. The gold that the girl acquires could be compared to the richness of the mind and the ability to have several points of view. The move to the depressive position gives her that.

What about the girl blackened by pitch? Does she remind us of fundamental human greed? In the underworld, the girl can meet the greedy, selfish, and envious part of herself. In the fairy tale, the girl has the courage to face that side of her, too. The tale ends with the words: "But the pitch clung fast to her, and could not be got off as long as she lived." This might be the human predicament: how to integrate those sides that do not fit with the ego ideal into the personality? We all have both good and bad qualities that we have to live with. The alternation of the bad destructive drives and the good, life-promoting, constructive drives goes on through life and it is what living is.

Men play a minor part in the three fairy tales chosen. They seem to be directed at girls, at least superficially. We can see the paranoid–schizoid and depressive positions vary in them all and, from that, we could conclude that they depict the eternal battle between good and bad, Eros and Thanatos. This is part of everybody's life and should, therefore, be accepted. *Mother Holle* depicts the relationship between the mother and daughter in which the daughter returns to earth from either the omnipotent mother figure or the oedipal father figure, to the mother who is both good and bad, who is disappointing but who also cares for her daughter, and also the one covered in black pitch as a symbol of evil. As a developmental result, the girl can return to the mother, identify with her, and separate from her again to continue her life outside the home, even if the developmentally earlier mother images have to be destroyed, as in *Little Snow-White*. It also requires courage that the girl obtains through identification with her father.

Is there a difference between boys and girls?

The big question is: what is the unconscious or conscious image that we have of the woman in our culture. Can we accept her as an independent actor with her own desires and goals? She needs to be able to use aggressive energy, power, and violence to do that. To be able to secure her own autonomy, the woman must draw a line between her own needs and the needs of the other: for instance, the needs of her child. She must be able to see the child as a separate other with her own needs. It is then possible for her to choose or give preference to either her own or the child's needs. Could the woman be allowed to hurt or violate the other when she adheres to her own wishes, or should she primarily think of the well-being of others? Or do we have to split the woman into the mother and the sexual woman or the career woman? Women fighting with the conflicts between the different desires blame themselves for not being able to be equally good enough in their roles of mothers, career women, and wives. It seems that they do not have the psychic right to make demands for themselves. The distress and shame caused by guilt feelings is often directed towards oneself in a woman. In the same kind of situation, men probably would direct their anger and violence against others.

The end

I'm not a Princess asleep,
I wake myself up
I kiss myself to wake me up.
I tell myself. Take up your bed and walk.
(Tiina Pystynen, 1987, translated for this edition)

References

Brown, L. M., Chesney-Lind, M., & Stein, N. (2007). Patriarchy matters: toward gendered theory of teen violence and victimization. *Violence Against Women, 13*(12): 1249–1273.

Euripides (1963). Medea. In: *Medea and Other Plays*, P. Wellacott (Trans.). London: Penguin.

Fonagy, P., Maran, G., & Target, M. (1992). Aggression and psychological self. *Bulletin of the Anna Freud Centre, 15*: 269–284.

Freud, S. (1913f). The theme of the three caskets. *S. E., 12*: 289–302. London: Hogarth.

Freud, S. (1923b). *The Ego and the Id. S. E., 19*: 3–66. London: Hogarth.

Freud, S. (1937c). Analysis terminable and interminable. *S. E., 23*: 209–253. London: Hogarth.

Goodkind, S., Wallace, J. M., Shook, J. J., Bachman, J., & O'Malley, P. (2009). Are girls really becoming more delinquent? Testing the gender convergence hypothesis by race and ethnicity, 1976–2005. *Child and Youth Service Review, 31*(8): 885–895.

Grimm, J., & Grimm, W. (1975). Mother Holle. In: *The Complete Grimm's Fairy Tales* (pp. 133–139). London: Routledge & Kegan Paul.

Grimm, J., & Grimm, W. (1975). Little Snow-White. In: *The Complete Grimm's Fairy Tales* (pp. 249–258). London: Routledge & Kegan Paul.

Grimm, J., & Grimm, W. (1999). Ruusunen (Sleeping Beauty). In: *Grimmin sadut I. Ruusunen* (pp. 118–123). Helsinki: Tammi.

Heide, K. M., & Solomon, E. P. (2009). Female juvenile murderers: biological and psychological dynamics leading to homicide. *International Journal of Law and Psychiatry, 32*(4): 244–245.

Ikonen, P., & Rechardt, E. (2004). *Thanatos, Shame and Other Essays.* London: Karnac.

Klein, M. (1946). Notes on some schizoid mechanisms. In: *Envy and Gratitude and Other Works 1946–1963* (pp. 1–24). London: Hogarth Press.

Ogden, T. H. (1990). *The Matrix of the Mind. Object Relations and the Psychoanalytic Dialogue.* Englewood Cliffs, NJ: Jason Aronson.

Perelberg, R. (1999). A core phantasy in violence. In: R. J. Perelberg (Ed.), *Psychoanalytic Understanding of Violence and Suicide* (pp. 89–108). London: Routledge.

Pystynen, T. (2006). I am not a Princess asleep. In: S. Ahola & S. Koskimies (Eds.), *Poems for Every Girl.* Hämeenlinna: Tammi.

CHAPTER SIX

Sister fantasy and sisterly love[1]

Elina Reenkola

P sychoanalytic literature thus far has not analysed the positive influence a sister has on a woman. Instead, a central theme has been sibling rivalry over the mother's love and the jealousy arising from this rivalry. A sister can rival, harass, or even torment a girl. Yet, a sister can also be an important ally. A girl can share the pains, conflicts, and secrets of growing up with her sister. Her sister can console her for the intolerable feelings resulting from separateness from, and loss of, the mother. A sister can become a substitute for the mother and an object of symbiotic longing. Indeed, identifications with big sisters can be essential in the formation of female identity. When the girl confronts the oedipal setting, allying herself with a sister can alleviate her feelings of being an outsider. Being similar in her body, being a girl and a child, a sister can lessen the girl's envy and feelings of inferiority in comparison to the adult sexual couple. In adolescence, a sister can reinforce the girl's developing independence and separateness.

Significantly, a girl can create an imaginary sister to alleviate her feelings of loneliness and exclusion. For example, in Astrid Lindgren's children's story *Most Beloved Sister* (2002), Barbro develops an imaginary sister, Ylva-Li, with whom she can share her thoughts and actions after her real little sister is born. The "most beloved sister" makes it easier for her to bear the loss of her mother's attention and love and her own feelings of being an outsider. This theme of twin beings as a tool for solidifying unstable identities has been explored by psychoanalysts interested in the problems of narcissism. In writing about twinship transference, Kohut (1971, p. 101) remarks that "the analysand needs and longs for the analyst, who reflects and reinforces, echoes and mirrors, the analysand's grandiose self".

A woman can create a fantasy of another woman as her sister. I have named this "sister fantasy". The inspiration to study sister fantasy came from the analysis of my patient Ada, who developed a sister fantasy in transference with me. At one point in her analysis, the poems of Edith Södergran were very meaningful to her, especially the poem "All the Echoes in the Forest", which describes losing one's sister to a man.

Inspired by this poem, I began to examine Edith Södergran's poems more closely. I found that in her set of seven poems titled "Fantastique", Edith Södergran uniquely describes a sister fantasy with her friend, the author Hagar Olsson.

Anna Freud developed a sister fantasy with her life companion, Dorothy Burlingham. I have reflected here on various the meanings of a sister fantasy for Ada, Edith, and Anna, and for women in general.

A sister fantasy may serve to complement a woman, to solidify her feminine identity, and to reflect a mirror image reinforcing her existence. The significance of the feeling of complementarity in lesbian love has been recognised (Burch, 1993; de Lauretis, 1999). I also pondered whether it is possible to create a sister fantasy as a transitional phenomenon in the space between separateness and symbiotic union in order to alleviate separation anxieties, or as a fetish-like phenomenon in order to deny an overly unbearable threat of separateness. Can the thought of a sister ease the shame and anxiety created by real or fantasied bodily imperfection (Reenkola, 2006)?

The analysis of Ada: your way of looking, my custom of listening

Let me illustrate further meanings of a sister fantasy with a glimpse of an analysis of a young woman, Ada, twenty-four years old.

In her analysis, Ada wanted to sit face-to-face, and she looked at me with relentless intensity four times a week. For a long time, Ada was not able to talk about the meaning of the eye contact. It was impossible for her to create symbols in words for the gaze. When I talked about eye contact, it meant for her that I forced her relinquish symbiotic desire and contact abruptly. If I did not stay with eye contact, she would go into fits of rage and throw my things around, especially at the ends of our sessions. She felt then that I tormented her without consideration for her agony. For her, giving up eye contact felt like falling into an abyss, into nothingness. My gaze meant the possibility of being loved. If I did not look at her intensely and incessantly, she felt she was repulsive, unlovable, abandoned, imperfect, and deficient. Inevitably, she was disappointed in me.

I often thought about my experiences of breast-feeding my own girl babies, the close unity of these situations, the shared warm drowsiness, as if merging together in a pleasurable feeling. I talked to Ada about longing for warm and pleasurable togetherness with me through eye contact. During moments of silence while being under Ada's intense gaze, I often thought about a little girl who desires her mother to hold her. A mother cannot say to her daughter, "You desire to get into my lap." Rather, the mother must pick up the girl and embrace her. How disappointed the girl would be if the mother did not do this. Having to content myself with expressing Ada's longing in words instead of satisfying it felt like cruelty, like sadistic torment. It was as if I had tormented her without consideration for her agony. She felt that I had lured her and seduced her, only to sadistically reject her. An analyst does not satisfy lap desire, but talks about it with empathic words and tones.

Ada was overcome by dark, inconsolable anguish at the thought of losing me, being separate from me. Melancholic gloominess varied with fits of rage for her first years in analysis when working through her loss of symbiotic love.

I felt like an acrobat moving carefully between the necessary disillusion of the symbiotic love and the equally necessary need to support a quota of the illusion of it.

My countertransference feelings and fantasies varied, indeed, from compassion to intolerable feelings. I felt that her gaze was controlling, penetrating, and sadistic. I felt as if I was a doll, under her dictatorship. Often, I felt like a prisoner without the freedom to look where I wanted. I felt her gaze as intolerably controlling and I had to work hard to contain it. I thought that Ada wanted to get inside my mind and brains just as in the film about John Malkovich (Jonze, 1999) that she often talked about. Sometimes, I escaped her gaze by planning a nice trip. I even tried to use my old reading glasses, with which I could see only one metre ahead. Thus, I tried to deal with intolerable countertransference feelings by acting out. This showed me how unendurable were the feelings Ada had had as a baby when she had no words or symbols for them. I also thought of a magic gaze that could reach the absent mother and reverse the early pain.

Little by little, we found out that Ada had experienced the birth of her sister when she was only thirteen months old as a sudden drastic loss of her mother's symbiotic love, and as a drop into horrifying emptiness, an abyss where words lost their meaning. The bridge to her mother was destroyed abruptly and cruelly. Significantly, her mother had spoken to her using long, perfectly correct sentences instead of babbling. This did not create the transitional space of cooing that is necessary for the baby to tolerate separateness. Later in her analysis, she was able to reconstruct and partly remember her mother's post partum depression after the birth of her sister. We began to understand together how intolerable were the experiences the little girl had had when losing the symbiotic love too suddenly and to feel compassion towards this little Ada and her suffering. She had not had enough feelings of primary narcissistic perfection and she desperately longed for this symbiotic fusion with mother.

Ada developed, in the third year of analysis, a sister fantasy; in her thoughts we were like sisters, not twins. Sister fantasy might become erotised. She thought of us in a tight embrace, face-to-face, with our arms, breasts, bellies, hips, and thighs touching and complementing each other. She described an intense yearning to caress me and my skin tenderly and to feel me caress her tenderly. Transiently, she found her ego ideal in me. Erotic transference manifested also as phallic strivings to penetrate me symbolically.

For a mother, it is natural to receive and understand the little girl's desire and longing for her, for the mother's embrace, skin contact, and the warmth of her body. I could understand an early longing for sensual touch and motherly sensuality. Yet, it was different and difficult to accept an adult woman's desire for me and for the caresses of my body. How could I handle and accept it in analysis, I wondered?

How different, indeed, is it from the physical touch between a mother and a little girl, from maternal desire? Homosexual libido is integrated in maternal desire and the mother's tender touch of her daughter. Yet, maternal desire and a woman's sexual desire are different.

In her fantasies, Ada had a lesbian orientation. She did not long for the difference of a man to complement herself, and, indeed, was disgusted by the male body.

In her fantasies and while masturbating, her sexual life was passionate. In the early stages of her analysis, while masturbating she would think of mechanical arousal, not of a human being. Later on, the object of her desire was a woman, one resembling herself. This woman might also use a dildo. Another fantasy was about a woman, who was dominating and sadistic. Four years later, she found a sexual partner, a woman of her own age.

In the third year of her analysis, during the long weekend starting with Ascension Day, Ada was suddenly overtaken by despair again. After the break, we talked about the following lines in Södergran's (1990) poem "All the Echoes in the Forest":

> No no no cry all the echoes in the forest:
> I have no sister.
> I go and lift up her white silk dress
> And embrace it powerlessly.
> I kiss you, all my passion I give to you.
> Can you recall her rosy limbs?
> Her shoes stand there in the sunshine,
> The gods warm their hands by them.
> Fall snow over my sister's remains,
> Whirl over them, snowstorm, your bitter heart
> With a shudder shall I approach this place
> As that unbearable spot where beauty was buried.
> (Södergran, 1990, p. 68, translated by Gounil Brown)

Ada wept quietly as she thought about these words. In her poem, Södergran writes about "a silken white dress" as a symbol for a wedding dress and her sister's wedding, when she loses her sister to a man. The poet describes this loss using metaphors of death. Losing me to the others—to my husband during the long weekend—felt like death to Ada. I talked about this to her. She was furious. She wanted to repudiate the significance of men. "I cannot understand how your object of desire can be a man!" she said. "Men are ugly brutes, why should one be in intimate contact with such creatures or have orgasms with them? A woman is much more beautiful and perfect!" she exclaimed.

She had split off the father's meaning as the provider of the mother's sexual satisfaction. At the same time, she spoke of the Law of the Father and the meaning of the phallus on a theoretical level, having carefully read her Kristeva and Lacan.

It was almost impossible for Ada to mourn the loss of symbiotic love or to create a symbol for the loss, to give it words, to create a transitional state with me.

The father as the object of love was impossible for her without, at the same time, losing the mother. The sister fantasy, thus, alleviated the desperation of the loss of mother and the intolerability of confronting the triangular oedipal setting. The sister fantasy was, at times, functioning as a fetish-like denial of separateness and physical inadequacy and, at other times, as a transitional state alleviating the separateness. The sister fantasy in my thoughts helped me to contain and bind Ada's erotic desire.

In order to be lovable, Ada had to be perfect. Only with brilliant intellectual and artistic achievements might she get the love she longed for. In my interpretation, her agony contained a fantasy of a sister analyst whose loss to a man during the weekend felt like death. The sister fantasy could alleviate the desperation of the loss of the symbiotic love. The magical annulment of separateness could also be maintained by the sister fantasy, as well as the illusion of perfection in confronting the triangular oedipal setting. She unconsciously tried to be a symbolic phallus to her mother and me, using her brilliant intellectual and artistic achievements.

During the fourth year of her analysis, Ada's relentless gaze subsided. The loss of symbiotic love gradually became tolerable for her. She made a psychic movement towards love of a man. She met Axel, with whom she experienced spiritual contact and a feeling of deep exaltation and sharing in the areas of art and science. Sexual desire for men, however, she renounced as impossible and dangerous. In a dream, she was alone with her mother in a bus travelling along a country road. Alongside the bus ran a donkey—a huge, translucent green, wild and free donkey. Powerfully and skilfully, the donkey swam across rivers that the bus crossed by means of bridges. Ada looked at the donkey with interest and curiosity, and asked her mother about it. Her mother did not answer and showed no interest in the donkey—a symbol of the father. This dream reflected Ada's experience of her father not being the object of her mother's desire or the one satisfying it. The donkey's wild power was tempting, but perilous. Ada associated the dream with her mother's depression, with death-like muteness, after the birth of her sister, maybe even earlier. In Ada's mind, the primal scene was mortally dangerous, as she blamed the father for her mother's deathlike depression. The move towards the father would also mean the loss of the vitally important mother for Ada. The man, nevertheless, remained alluring to her.

The frightening danger of the primal scene was similarly reflected in a dream Ada had the following weekend. In her dream, Axel was glancing under the hem of her miniskirt. Ada associated Axel's sexual interest in her with the shipwreck of the passenger ferry *Estonia*. Physical arousal and pleasure with a man was frightening to her, threatening her ego with destruction and death. Eros and Thanatos, sexual interest and death, are linked together in Ada's mind. In her dream, a female friend appeared as a sister. The sister fantasy here served as a frail but protective bridge.

Ada suffered under the torment of her sexual desires. Her sexual passion was directed towards a woman, yet she longed for spiritual and intellectual union with a man. In her unconscious, a sexual relationship with a man was life threatening.

Towards the end of the fourth year of analysis, Ada, for the first time, dared to experience sexual pleasure with another person. She met a woman who was interested in her, respected her, and desired her. It was a relief for her to dare to share sexual pleasure with another person and to feel mutual affection and compassion. It alleviated her unconscious fears about being overpowered or intruded upon by another person, and consolidated herself. It became easier for her to concentrate on her intellectual and artistic work, and alongside this absorption in her work, she also dared to enjoy her moments of relaxation more.

For Ada, the sister fantasy signified a transitional state which alleviated her sorrow over the loss of the mother and consolidated her femininity. At times, it was also a fetish-like construct with which she was able to deny the loss of the mother, evade the resulting sorrow, and maintain the illusion of symbiotic fusion. It also allowed her to sustain the illusion of bodily perfection and alleviated her feelings of shame. Thus, she was able to deny the significance of the man's penis in satisfying the desire of the mother/woman. In Ada's fantasies, the phallus was transferable—it could be transferred to a woman. A transferable phallus could be realised in dazzling intellectual and artistic feats. A man was not needed for this.

Like Ada, Edith Södergran also developed an elaborate sister fantasy, which functioned in rather similar ways. Let us examine how Södergran's sister fantasy manifests itself in her poems.

Edith Södergran

Edith Södergran (1892–1923) was one of the pioneers of modern, Swedish-language Finnish poetry. Hagar Olsson was an author, editor, and founding member of the modernist journal *Ultra*. Their intense friendship began in 1919. The poet died at the age of thirty-one, virtually unknown. In 1986, Hagar Olsson published a volume of Edith Södergran's letters with her own commentary, both of which demonstrate that their "sisterhood" was significant and inspiring to both of them, especially to the infirm Edith who, not having any siblings, led a lonely and secluded life with her mother.

I interpret Södergran's poems, from a psychoanalytic perspective, as a stream of consciousness produced by the author, as thoughts about her own experiences. A limitation inherent in this applied form of psychoanalysis used for analysing literature, films, or other works of art is that, unlike in a normal psychoanalytic setting, the author is not available to validate or refine the interpretations. Thus, they remain hypothetical suggestions. Another danger is that the theory itself shapes how we look at a literary text.

Edith Södergran's poems and letters to Hagar Olsson depict, in a sensitive and emotional way, a friendship between two women, their deep attachment and erotic charge. In Olsson, Edith found a sister and a playmate, after being disappointed by a man in her longing to find love. In her comments on Edith's letters, Hagar Olsson describes how she experienced Edith's affection as something complementary, as rapture and enchantment. She, too, had long yearned for a language of sisters, for people who would understand each other deeply and feel themselves to be of one heart and one soul. Together, Edith and Hagar dreamed about a new human existence, conscious of its calling. They had both independently embarked upon this quest, and found in each other a kindred spirit. They dreamed of establishing contacts with other kindred spirits in Europe and the world. In Edith's letters to Hagar, there is a powerful current of erotic longing and the exalted feeling of falling in love, as well as jealous disappointment when Hagar is unable to devote herself to her alone.

Mother, father, and the primal scene

I have attempted to outline Edith's inner world by interpreting her biographical information, her letters, and her poetry. Edith grew up as an only child, with a devoted, strong mother who was interested in literature and suffrage issues, and a father who was becoming an alcoholic, and who was also weak, less educated, and ill. In 1907, Edith's father, Matts Södergran, died of tuberculosis after being sick for three years. Edith was fifteen at the time, and fell ill with tuberculosis a year later.

Edith was named after the initial letters of her brother Edvard, who had died when he was eighteen days old. The child's father had left Edith's mother, Helen Holmroos, and married another. Edvard had also been the name of Edith's mother's little brother, who had died at the age of one. Both Edvards, the dead little brother and the dead love-child of youth, continued their lives in the first two letters of Edith's name, thus illustrating her mother's difficulty in working through the sorrow of an intolerable loss and remaining fixated on the dead. Giving the name of a dead baby to a new baby often reflects the wish that the dead one would continue its life in the new baby and would, thus, compensate for the loss. In any case, Edith had to carry a reminder of the dead baby and the loss of the dead baby's father in the initials of her name, probably reflecting some of the unmourned loss of the poet's mother and, perhaps, her grandmother as well.

Owing to the mother's grief not being mourned, the daughter might unconsciously assume the task of healing the mother's sorrow and repairing her narcissistic wound, and might sacrifice other channels of striving for pleasure on the altar of the mother's well-being. The child might start to maintain the vitality of the depressed mother and could devote herself to nourishing her, as if she alone were responsible for it (Green, 1986). "I am just one among many, and others are stronger than I, I am the shield they will look to, I am the core and the uniting link" Södergran writes (1984, p. 169). This might symbolise Edith's fantasy of healing her mother. Meanings cathected to the depressed mother can dramatically influence the working-through of the oedipal setting (Green, 1986).

Being the object of her mother's devotion and her only source of satisfaction can hinder a girl's separation from a symbiotic love of her mother. If the father does not function as the third, as the object of desire in the mother's mind, it might prevent the girl's reaching out towards loving the father and separating from the mother. It is then impossible for the girl to identify with the mother as a sexual woman desiring the father. The relationship between the mother and the daughter possibly became so seamless that it allowed no room for a sexual woman growing into adulthood. Such a close-knit relationship is not likely to mirror to the girl an accepting image of the mother as a separate and different girl and woman.

In her status as the only, pampered daughter, Edith became used to being the centre of her mother's life. Her early poetry provides glimpses of her father's lesser importance and the mother "queen's" mitigating stance towards him. The father does not seem to live as the object of desire in her mother's mind. Her position as the primary object of her mother's attention might be the biographical background for her feelings of superiority, grandiosity, and omnipotence that shine through many of Edith's poems. She had a certain grandiose faith in herself and her potential as a forerunner, as a pioneer. In her prophetic poems, she describes herself as a Nietzschean superman, as the temple priestess, the flame of the future.

Devoting herself to her efforts to revive her depressed mother, the daughter might remain fixated on her. The change of the object of love from mother to father can become impossible and dangerous for the girl, if she fears it means losing the mother's love.

The primal scene shakes a girl's illusion of perfection. The thought of a father who can also fulfil the mother's desire, and can even revive the depressed mother and bring her orgiastic pleasure, thoroughly shakes the foundations of the daughter's narcissistic omnipotence. The consequence may be erotic and aggressive de-libidinalisation of the primal scene to the advantage of intense intellectual activity. This way of dealing with the issue restores the girl's wounded narcissism by sacrificing libidinal satisfaction. Artistic creativity can gain impetus from this setting and help alleviate narcissistic wounds (Green, 1986).

The false mirror

The search for a mirror image is a central repeated element in Söder-gran's poems. The poet is disappointed in the love of a man and the mirror image he provides, for the mirror he provides distorts and destroys. The man is a false mirror that the woman hurls against the cliffs in rage, as she writes in her poem "Violetta skymningar" [Violet Twilight]. Similarly, in the poem "Kärlek" [Love] (Södergran, 1992), a mirror provided by a man reflects disease and crumbling.

> I left it on a rock by the sea and naked I came to you, looking like a woman. And like a woman I sat at your table and drank a toast in wine, inhaling the scent of some roses. You found me beautiful, like something you saw in a dream. I forgot everything, I forgot my child-hood and my country, I only knew that your caresses held me captive. Smiling, you held up a mirror and asked me to look. I saw that my shoulders were made of dust and crumbled away, I saw that my beauty was sick and wished only to disappear. Oh, hold me in tight in your arms so close that I need nothing. (p. 71)

This poem tells a touching story of the threat of disintegration, crumbling, and vanishing resulting from the reflection of the false mirror. The poet is insecure about her femininity; she comes "looking like a woman", not unequivocally as a woman. The beautiful mirror image reflected in the man's eyes turns into an image that reflects her beauty as imperfect, sick, and incomplete. The mirror image provided by the man disintegrates her illusion of perfection. Her feeling of femi-nine beauty crumbles and the integrity of her bodily ego vanishes. The poet hopes that a tight, symbiotic embrace would save her from the threat of disintegration and would restore the feeling of perfection that she longs for, the experience that "I need nothing".

Behind the false mirror provided by the man can be the experience of an earlier mirror, that provided by the mother's face. This mirror is central to the consolidation of the baby's self. In Winnicott's (1971, p. 111) theory of the mother's role as a mirror, the baby looks at the mother's face and sees himself. If the baby does not see herself reflected in the mother's face, but, rather, sees the reflection of the mother's own mood or the mother's face set in a rigid defence, the result for the baby can be the threat of chaos and disintegration. Edith Södergran depicts such chaos and disintegration in her poem "Kärlek" [Love], which tells about the false mirror image reflected by the man.

For Södergran, man in all his difference is not only a longed-for complement, the fulfiller of the throbbing inner space, but also a heart-rending disappointment and the highlighter of her own imperfection.

Edith and Hagar: sister love and sisterly love

Edith Södergran's and Hagar Olsson's intense friendship, which, on an intellectual and spiritual level, also became an erotic love affair, began in January 1919, immediately after Södergran's response to Olsson's review of her poem collection *Septemberlyran* [The September Lyre]. For both of them, finding a "soul mate" was a powerful experience, filled with rapture and enchantment.

In her first letter to Hagar Olsson, before meeting her in person, Edith Södergran writes, "could we talk to one another in a divine way, so that all barriers fall down? And are you the sea of fire I would like to throw myself into?" (Olsson, 1990, p. 93). The longing for a merging, symbiotic love with no boundaries or barriers was immediately evoked in the poet, and elicited a similar response in Hagar Olsson. In her reply, she comments, "I cannot describe the joy I felt when I received the letter. It was a joy which touched my innermost core, that area in my innermost core where I was most lonely." Hagar had never before opened up her innermost core to anyone, and had lived with a hunger "which probably could never be satisfied" (p. 27). Later she writes,

> And in addition, there was the enchantment which naturally emerged between Edith and me. I cannot use any other word; it was a magical kind of rapture which overtook us and created an atmosphere where everything seemed possible and anything could happen. (Olsson, 1990, p. 44)

Like Edith, Hagar also fostered hopes about giving birth "to a new kind of human being". "This perspective contained a subtle and faint intoxication, intellectual joy and secret excitement which, together with our girlishly intense infatuation with each other made our shared time a feast, soft and dreamy as the spring itself."

Around the same time, soon after the two had become acquainted, Edith Södergran wrote in a letter,

> I have a sister, and I have not heard her wonderful voice—I want to see your innermost core, your Holy of Holies.—I shall write a love-letter to you, Hagar, when I am in that mood. Now I have one who is mine, for the whole of my life. Two years ago I wrote a poem. Each stanza began with the words: I wish to have a playmate, and the poem ended with the words: I wish to have a playmate, who breaks out of the dead granite to defy eternity. Now this joyous playmate exists, after a two-year wait (Olsson, 1990, pp. 31–32)

She finally found a playmate, after longing for one for many years. Note, however, that at first she had longed for a male playmate, but now she found a female one."

Södergran and Olsson met for the first time some time later, in early February of the same year, at the poet's home in Raivola. At the end of February, Södergran writes, "Hagar kissed me once. There was more in that kiss than words can tell, it contained a shocking, small medical record" (Olsson, 1990, p. 49). Passionate infatuation is reflected in her letters from that spring.

> Hagar, you are a sick child. Come into my arms as into the arms of a mother. I feel in myself the power which can vanquish your enemies, let me rule you. Surrender yourself to my will, to the sun, the life-force to prana. (Olsson, 1990, p. 50)

She herself had been ill with tuberculosis for over ten years already, but nevertheless felt powerful vitality, which Hagar also experienced in her whole being. She called Hagar by the nickname "gyllene barn", the golden child. The poet describes Hagar's "golden locks" with tender words. It is impossible to know whether their relationship remained platonic friendship and love, although the electrified lesbian eroticism of her poems and letters might also indicate a physical love relationship. Were Södergran's powerful erotic images only fantasies and longings, which were then transformed into fairy-tale-like fuel for creative writing and transposed into the power and tension of poetry without being physically fulfilled? We shall never know.

Although they only met a total of five times during their four-and-a-half year friendship, these meetings sufficed to fuel the poet's passionate friendship. She waited for Hagar's visits, and wrote that her blood flowed hotter when she thought of her. The meetings were inspiring and happy. Hagar Olsson was her sister soul, her literary supporter, critic, adviser, and her only friend. Olsson helped the poet get her poems published.

Södergran's set of poems entitled *Fantastique* contains seven sister poems which were inspired by Hagar Olsson. In her letter to Olsson, she wrote,

> I have thought that the sister-set could be called 'Fantastique.' Are you happy with that name? Thank you for all the trouble you have seen on behalf of the book. I hope that no one will be able to guess who the sister is. Be crafty, behave in such a manner that the Schildts would not be able to guess anything. (Olsson, 1990, p. 62)

The seven *Fantastique* poems tell the poet's love story with Hagar Olsson. The set begins with their first meeting in spring, tells about the fulfilment of this impossible love, about emerging jealousy, fears of loss, and, finally, ends with forebodings about Hagar's departure and their parting of ways.

The fourth poem, which Ada also found touching, "Alla ekon i skogen" [All the Echoes in the Forest] (Södergran 1990) crystallises some of the most central conflicts and longings Edith has with the sister:

> No no no cry all the echoes in the forest:
> I have no sister.
> I go and lift up her white silk dress
> And embrace it powerlessly.
> I kiss you, all my passion I give to you.
> Can you recall her rosy limbs?
> Her shoes stand there in the sunshine,
> The gods warm their hands by them.
> Fall snow over my sister's remains.
> Whirl over them, snowstorm, your bitter heart
> With a shudder shall I approach this place
> As that unbearable spot where beauty was buried.
>
> (Södergran, 1990, p. 68)

In the poem, the loss of the sister to a man is likened to death, and the attempt to undo it with a negation—"No no no"—fails. At the time of the writing, Hagar was engaged to R. R. Eklund, although the relationship was ending. The silken white dress can be interpreted as symbolising a wedding gown and marriage to a man. If the object of the sister's desire was a man, this would destroy the love and affection between the sisters. Powerlessly, the poet embraces the silk dress. The sister has been taken by a man, the wielder of phallic power. Observations about woman's bodily imperfection, powerlessness, and phallic castration culminate in a comparison with masculine power and potency. The man is a superior rival in the competition for the sister's love. The poet is forced to bury "beauty", the illusion about the female body's perfection. Confronting "ugliness", that is, the castrated and inadequate body, is likened to death, the "unbearable spot where beauty was buried". A wedding celebration with a man leads to the sister's death; in the poet's primal scene fantasy, the woman is destroyed and dies. This scene probably repeats the horrors of losing her mother and her attempt to deny the loss, as well as repeating the primal stage where the mother is destroyed together with the father. For her, a sexual relationship between a man and a woman contains mortal danger and death.

The seventh poem, "Gudabarnet" [The Child of God] (Södergran, 1984), tells of a divine child, Hagar, who sits with the poet while she sings a song with a golden lyre. The setting creates an intense feeling of intimacy. Playing the golden lyre is a picturesque metaphor for the erotic charge between the women. Playing the lyre can also be a symbol of the woman's libido, female orgasm, which features a spreading vibration rather than the sudden burst of the man's orgasm. The poem also reflects a foreboding about Hagar's departure to go elsewhere, and the sorrow of parting.

> The child of god sat with me. The gold lyre sang out of my hands. The child of god stares out into unending dusks. The song circles over her head on broad wings. What do you see in the song? It is your own future that heaves itself Out of icy dusks, Your own binding, calling, waiting future. (Södergran, 1984, p. 73)

In addition to their fairy-tale-like charm and erotic charge, this set of poems also contains glimpses of passionate eroticism, possessiveness, and jealousy. The sister is a beautiful, divine child with golden locks, rosy arms, and silken clothes. There is no room for a third in the close, unifying understanding and love between two women. A narcissistic component is an important strand in sister fantasy here.

Can a woman, in contrast to a man, provide a reflecting mirror? In Hagar, Edith sees the real mirror image, someone with whom to share her secrets and to listen to her. Hagar's mirror provides the complementing reflection of a sister, a narcissistic love for someone like herself.

The demands the poet made on Hagar, as well as her jealous longing for possessive love, strengthened as their friendship continued. It was hard for Edith to tolerate Hagar's lively social life and human relationships in Stockholm and elsewhere in the world, and between the lines she was hurt by them. In her letters, the poet, with demanding curiosity, pesters Hagar for details about all her friends. In the commentary Hagar Olsson later wrote on Edith's letters, irritation and anger towards the poet's demanding nature begin to emerge. A little over four years after their friendship began, Hagar Olsson travelled to Southern Europe in the spring of 1923. Edith Södergran died in the summer of the same year at the age of thirty-one.

"How wonderful that you get to go to the sweet south", the poet wrote in April 1923. She urged Hagar to "forget us completely for the duration of the trip". Bravely, the poet tried to deny the painful feelings of loss, disappointment, and abandonment which Hagar's trip and "being forgotten" brought her. However, she admits to having melancholy feelings of longing: "I already miss you, I feel in my belly that something benevolent and warm is withdrawing, distancing itself".

Hagar Olsson did not publish Edith's letters to her until twenty-five years after her death, after much hesitation. Reading the letters again, twenty-five years after Edith's death, had been very painful to her. She had consciously tried to bury them and thus seal away "the most bitter experience of my youth", the death of Edith. Re-reading the letters was so painful to her that she likens the experience to surgery in which your heart is slashed open. Feelings of guilt for having embarked on a long journey to Europe without first having gone to see the poet despite her pleas to do so tormented her. Edith had indeed experienced Hagar's leaving for the trip as an inconsolable abandonment. Desperate feelings of guilt over this "abandonment" of the poet and over her death led Hagar to consider ending her own life.

After the poet's death, she received from her mother a small piece of the cover of a notebook which had the poet's last words to Hagar written on it: "Has she forgotten me Hagar are we not united to each other in life and in death—".

Edith seemed to have had the illusion that she and Hagar were united eternally. She was shocked when she realised that Hagar had other important people in her life, bringing "the third" into their union. A little child has the same illusion in the symbiotic union with mother. The existence of a third may abruptly end the blissful union. It might feel like a deathly catastrophe to the child. In Edith, the lethal illness indeed overpowered her during the summer that Hagar left her.

Anna Freud and Dorothy Burlingham

Just as a sister fantasy can provide a positive mirror enabling a woman to realise her own femininity, as we saw with Edith and Hagar, a sister fantasy can also help to fill the void created by an absent mother. This we can see in the example of Anna Freud and Dorothy Burlingham.

Anna Freud found a friend in Dorothy Burlingham after the latter moved to Vienna in 1925 with her four children to get help for her son's psychological problems, as Elizabeth Young-Bruehl records in Anna Freud's biography (Young-Bruehl, 1998). Anna and Dorothy created a sister fantasy with each other, and derived joy and contentment from it. In their letters, both of them happily describe this twin-sister fantasy. Dorothy Burlingham actually had twin older sisters. In her letters to Anna Freud, she writes how a sister of twins often creates a fantasy twin, to complement herself. The fantasy twin represents, in Dorothy's mind, the ideal self. They mirrored each other.

Anna was born to the Freud family as the sixth and youngest child. Her mother, Martha, was exhausted after the delivery and did not have the energy to tend her youngest child herself, but she did not get her a wetnurse, as she had done for Martin, the older brother. Responsibility for Anna's care was taken up by the family's nursemaid, Josefine Cihlarz. Josefine's and Anna's relationship was very close, as attested in the following story told by Anna. When she was little, they were out in a park and Anna lost sight of Josefine for a moment. In a panic, Anna had gone searching for her, even though her mother was right there.

Now Anna in turn got lost, and was found in the park only after a long search. Anna Freud used this event as the basis for her essay "On losing and being lost". There she writes how "It is . . . or when the mother's emotions are temporarily engaged elsewhere that children not only feel lost but, in fact, get lost" (Young-Bruehl, 1998, p. 34). "As a child, Dorothy Burlingham had felt, as Anna Freud had, like an unwanted hanger-on in her household, a little one who was a bore and nuisance to the older ones" (Olsson, 1990, p. 62).

The feeling of being lost which Anna Freud describes can contain early experiences of the mother's absence, which can be caused by the mother's depression or exhaustion. When the little child all of a sudden does not find the mother, feelings of panic and chaos are evoked. This experience is on the same dimension as Winnicott's description of a child who cannot find himself reflected in his mother's expression, as this, too, can lead to a feeling of disintegration. Edith Södergran expresses this experience in her poem "Love".

Anna's friendship with, and sister fantasy about, Dorothy probably helped Anna to find something that was her own and reinforced her femininity—the kind of love and compassion she had not received from her mother or sisters. In her letters, she described longing for something for herself, "Etwas-Haben-Wollen". For her, this felt like a shameful dependency that she concealed even from her father in her analysis with him.

Anna did not have a solid path to femininity as a result of her close relationship with her idolised father, the way she identified with him, adopted his theories and profession, went through analysis with him, coupled with her distant relationship with her mother. Anna, whom her father called Antigone, would have remained in the "Antigone's grave" defined by her possessive father if not for her friendship with Dorothy. For Anna, who had turned her back on her mother and compensated by limiting her life to adopting and continuing the pioneering work of her idolised father as a daughter solely devoted to him, allying herself with Dorothy might have helped her in her longings for complementarity.

There were rumours in psychoanalytic circles that Anna and Dorothy had a lesbian relationship, but her biographer, Young-Bruehl (1988), concludes that she remained "vestal": she did not have a sexual relationship with Dorothy or anyone else. Anna and Dorothy lived together and shared their life for fifty years. How close their friendship was can be seen in how, after Dorothy died in 1979, Anna consoled herself by wrapping herself in her friend's shirts and stroking them movingly, although no one had ever seen them hugging while Dorothy lived (Young-Bruehl, 1988).

Denied or repressed sexuality can be rediscovered either symbolically or through another person, in a complementing, supplementary relationship. This is how Anna Freud described male homosexual relationships in her lectures that were never published. Many theorists have emphasised the significance of the feeling of complementarity in lesbian love (e.g., Burch, 1989; de Lauretis, 1999). An element of longing for complementarity can also exist in friendships between women and in heterosexual love. In a twin, and also in a sister, one can see another complementing oneself, one's ideal self, as it were. This might be the case in Anna's sister fantasy with Dorothy.

The loss of paradise

The loss of the symbiotic mother and primary narcissism may feel like expulsion from paradise. For a depressed person, mourning the loss of the mother remains impossible. For Ada, the early loss of the mother and maternal depression were painful. For Anna, the absent mother was intolerable. Edith was not able to separate from her mother, lethal illness strengthening the bond between them. In turn, if the mother is depressed, the child keeps the "dead mother" (Green, 1986) in a burial chamber, unable to give her up. If one refuses to lose the mother, one cannot imagine her or name her. The depressed person is painfully stuck with an object s/he refuses to lose. This non-loss, non-symbolisation, is often present in the psychotic. With language and symbols, we can attempt to create a bridge to the lost, absent mother (Segal, 1957). After accepting the loss of mother and mourning it, we can rediscover the mother through language and symbols. An artist may fuse together this kind of non-symbolic language and the strivings of an omnipotent self, moving between the painful sorrow of losing the mother and the omnipotence of holding on to the mother. Here, language can act as an antidote for depression, a survival tool, an attempt to escape psychotic depression, "the black sun of melancholy" written about by the French nineteenth-century poet Nerval (Kristeva, 1998).

Transitional states and fetishes

As we have seen in these examples, a woman can create a sister fantasy both in a transitional state serving as a bridge to separateness, and as a fetish to deny separateness and the feelings of imperfection.

A transitional object is created for dealing with separateness (Winnicott 1971). Similarly, a fetish can also be created to deal with separateness, alongside its purpose of dealing with lack and castration anxiety.

The meaning of an unconscious sister fantasy changed during Ada's analytic process. The agony of separateness could be alleviated by means of a sister fantasy. The illusion of perfection when confronting the primal scene and the oedipal triangle could also be maintained by using the sister fantasy as a fetish. The fantasy could alleviate her feelings of shame.

The sister fantasy in Edith's poetry remained solid and fixed. She could rediscover bodily perfection and integrity through her fantasy of a sister. A mirror image of one like herself strengthened her identity and alleviated her shame about "that unbearable spot where beauty was buried". Of course, we only have her written fantasies available.

For Anna, the sister fantasy with Dorothy might have helped her to find the love and compassion she did not get from her absent mother.

Sometimes, a fetish can develop out of transitional objects (Winnicott, 1971). Freud (1927e) has described the fetish in the following way. The boy experiences panic when he perceives his mother's genitals and thinks that she has been castrated and that the same fate could threaten him. When the boy creates a fetish, he uses it to confront his castration anxiety sothrough disavowal and the splitting of the ego into two. The fetish allows for the simultaneous existence of two opposite, mutually exclusive ideas: the idea that a woman does not have a penis and, simultaneously, that a woman does have a penis. Freud specifically emphasised that a fetish is a boy's creation for dealing with castration anxiety. He thought that the girl was already castrated and, thus, did not have castration anxiety in the same sense.

Dealing with castration anxiety is preceded by dealing with the loss of the mother with the same mechanisms, and, contrary to what Freud thought, a woman can also create a fetish (Chasseguet-Smirgel,

1985; Greenacre, 1969; McDougall, 1980). The child can process the intolerable loss of the mother and separation from her through denial and splitting, and also by creating a fetish, with which she attempts to maintain unity with mother. In dealing with separation anxiety, a fetish allows for the magical annulment of separation and separateness while simultaneously, through the splitting of the ego, allowing the opposite feeling of the separateness of the mother and the child.

The vicissitudes of a girl's love are different from those of a boy, because she changes the love object from mother to father in heterosexual development. The girl's first love ends in disappointment. The girl can never become like the father or satisfy mother's desire, which is also at the core of a girl's shame. A girl's childhood wishes to possess the mother in the negative oedipal position are often ultimately shameful and buried deep in the unconscious. In confronting the primal scene, where the father satisfies the mother's desire, the girl's narcissism suffers a severe blow. The girl is likely to suffer a serious defeat in her first love affair and might register this defeat as being due to her inadequacy. She is rejected for her genitals. This is a serious blow to a girl's narcissism. The fetish helps her to deal with her imperfection and heal her wounds.

If the loss of the mother and the experience of separateness have remained intolerable, confronting castration anxiety might evoke powerful anxiety over the frailty of one's body. Confronting and dealing with separation anxiety and castration anxiety with these mechanisms alternates continuously as a dialectical process. A fetish can symbolise the breast alongside of, instead of, or with, the phallus. The creation of a fetish enables sexual satisfaction despite the dangers threatening the fragile body image. Disavowal of the primal scene is central in the creation of a fetish. The primal scene is the greatest threat to the girl's wish to possess her mother.

Lesbian loves

Every female has sensual experiences of her mother's body, starting from the womb. Mother is the first object of love and desire for the girl. However, the little girl has to give up her desire to be the sole object of mother's love and devotion.

The two poles of a libido with a lesbian orientation originate in the childhood desire to possess the mother and the creative power and fertility of her inner space, as well as striving to be like the father and to attain his genital equipment and its symbolic power and potency (McDougall, 1995). After turning away from this original dual goal, the homosexual libido can find various paths and ways of bringing them together which can either enrich or undermine the self. The girl can incorporate into herself the vicissitudes and economic practices of lesbo–phallic desire, and invest this vitally important libidinal energy as her fuel in the areas of love relationships, professional and creative aspirations, or motherhood. There can be many kinds of conflicts and problems in transforming lesbian libido and integrating it into the self, and they can be a source of both creativity and neurotic problems. Both women with a lesbian orientation and those with a heterosexual orientation encounter problems in integrating the homosexual libido into the self.

In lesbian love, the object of a woman's desire is a woman. Freud (1920a) wrote about homosexuality in his article about the psychogenesis of a homosexual woman. This is the only case of female homosexuality that Freud reports. The case has no name, unlike Freud's other cases. Freud describes the girl's negative transference, hostility, and contempt towards him, but he was not able to contain it or deal with it. He realises that the patient has transferred to him "the sweeping repudiation of men which had dominated her ever since the disappointment she had suffered from her father" (p. 164). Freud breaks off the treatment when the girl developed a negative transference towards him and advises that she should resume it with a woman analyst. Instead of containing the girl's repudiation and hostility towards him and verbalising it in empathic words, Freud acted in an aggressive way, breaking off the treatment and leaving the case nameless. I think leaving the case nameless was Freud's unconscious revenge on this eighteen-year-old girl. He recognises the girl's "yearning for a kinder mother" and "the search for a substitute mother to whom she could become passionately attached", but does not dwell on this issue with the girl.

Freud made noteworthy statements about homosexuality in the article: he wrote about the universal bisexuality of human beings, "in all of us, throughout the life, the libido normally oscillates between male and female objects". He called homosexuality inversion, not perversion. The homosexual girl in his case was not pathological. She had no neurotic conflicts. She had passed through the normal feminine Oedipus complex. Object choice and identification do not necessarily coincide. Three sets of characteristics vary independently of one another: object choice, mental sexual characters, and physical sexual characters. The chain of causation can be recognised with certainty in analysis afterwards, but to predict it is impossible. It is not for psychoanalysis to solve the problem of homosexuality.

The girl's identity was later discovered: her name was Sidonie Czillag and she died at the age of 100 in 1990. According to her biographers, Ines Rieder and Diana Voigt (2000), she had lived an eventful life.

Jacques André (2013) also suggests multiple psychogenesis for homosexuality. Homosexuality is the result of different psychic histories and psychic determination combines different sources. It is more accurate to speak about homosexualities in plural, indeed. It makes sense to talk about lesbianism or lesbian loves in plural.

In her theory of lesbian desire, de Lauretis (1999) attempts to chart the ways and "psychogenesis" of a desire that exceeds and eludes the confines of the oedipal script with the help of a post oedipally created fetish. The female equivalent of castration is the woman's perception of an inadequate or unlovable body image, her whole body. Here, de Lauretis uses the term "female castration" to describe the woman's experience of the inadequacy of her feminine body. This is a wider formulation of female castration than the two forms commonly proposed, woman's phallic castration complex (anxiety over bodily inadequacy due to the lack of a penis) and feminine castration anxiety (anxiety over damage to female genitals or babies and fertility). Just as the man who creates a fetish disavows his observation of castration, the woman in turn might disavow her observation that her body might be imperfect or unlovable for her parents. The woman creating a fetish disavows her observation and utilises the splitting of the ego to simultaneously maintain two mutually exclusive notions: she is perfect and she is not perfect. In this setting, finding the lost ideal self and perfect body in another woman is the essential dynamic in a woman's love for a woman. The object of the woman's lesbian love would, thus, not be her mother's body or her father's phallus, but her own body, the sense of perfection of which she has lost. This lost illusion of a perfect body she can re-discover in fantasy and with another woman. According to de Lauretis's argument, the issue is a "post oedipal disavowal" of one's bodily imperfection, where the subject whose desire is lesbian has gone through the Oedipus complex but, as a result of disavowing lack and castration, her desire is attached to a fetish object, to one like herself. The fetish object is the object of both narcissistic love and object love, engaging at once both object libido and ego libido (de Lauretis 1999).

In psychoanalytic theory, the phallus signifies the symbolic value and meaning of the penis. The phallus can be detached and transferred (Freud, 1917c), and symbolises power, worth, potency, and productivity. A moveable phallus that can be transferred is central to the study of lesbian love, according to Butler (1995). The lesbian phallus takes the role of repairing bodily inadequacy as a fetish. Phallic desire is manifested as a power seeking to penetrate the innermost core or to push itself outwards, or to dominate. In the area of the intellect, it is also manifested as penetrating new areas without prejudice and with curiosity, in the form of analysing, clearing away hurdles and doing pioneering work. The tone and reach of the "lesbian gaze" is phallic, penetrating and shamelessly inquisitive, and this it does knowingly. The gaze is directed deep into the core of the object. In concrete terms, the lesbian phallus can be a dildo. A lesbian phallus as the location of desire would, thus, not signify identification with a man or masculine desire, the search for a penis. Rather, it would signify the idea that gender, and more specifically, the masculine "hegemonic symbolical gender structure", is transferable. The transferrable phallus could be a dazzling intellectual achievement or artistic creation used as a fetish, as we could see in Ada's analysis.

Perfect or lovable

The fragile and shameful body image was a crucial issue for both Edith and Ada. Being bodily "imperfect", only one sex and not omnipotent, had the catastrophic meaning of not being loved by the mother. A narcissistic illusion of beauty and perfection could be reached by creating a sister fantasy. Only perfection would mean lovability.

In a sister fantasy, a woman may find a mirror image of herself and use it to strengthen her identity, repair her narcissistic wounds, and alleviate her shame. Allying with a sister can significantly alleviate the humiliation and shame inherent in the oedipal setting. Bodily similarity with the sister empowers a woman and brings her feelings of perfection and integrity, alleviating castration anxiety, both for heterosexual and lesbian women. A sister fantasy can be created as a transitional phenomenon where it eases the transition into separateness and accepting otherness. As a fetish-like defence against the pain of losing one's mother, the sister fantasy can also be used to deny separateness and maintain the illusion of a symbiotic union.

Edith Södergran, Anna Freud, and Ada were able to seek a complementing reflection in a sister fantasy. Complementarity can be applied to many kinds of relationship, sexual or not. In the close friendships of girls and women, the sister fantasy, sisterhood of the soul, sisterly love is present as one strand in a sublimated form, mutually complementing and reinforcing femininity. In her poem "Sorger" [Sorrows], Edith Södergran (1984) tells us to turn to our sister and to talk to one another about our secrets:

> You will show me your beauty and your way of looking
> And I shall offer you my silence and my custom of listening
>
> (p. 135)

Note

1. Translated by Kimmo Absetz and Nely Keinänen.

References

André, J. (2013). Masculine homosexualities in psychoanalysis today. Unpublished paper presented on 31 May to the Istanbul IPA/COWAP Conference on Homosexualities.

Burch, B. (1993). Gender identities, lesbianism, and potential space. *Psychoanalytic Psychology*, 10: 359–375.

Butler, J. (1993). *Bodies that Matter*. New York: Routledge.

Chasseguet-Smirgel, J. (1985). *The Ego Ideal*. London: Free Association Books.

De Lauretis, T. (1999). Letter to an unknown woman. In: R. C. Lesser & E. Schoenberg (Eds.), *That Obscure Subject of Desire*. New York: Routledge.

Freud, S. (1917c). On the transformation of instinct, as exemplified in anal erotism. *S. E.*, *17*: London: Hogarth.

Freud, S. (1920a). The psychogenesis of a case of homosexuality in a woman. S. E., *18*: London: Hogarth.

Freud, S. (1927e). Fetishism. *S. E.*, *21*: London: Hogarth.

Green, A. (1986). *On Private Madness*. Madison, CT: International Universities Press.

Greenacre, P. (1969). The fetish and the transitional object. *Psychoanalytic Study of the Child*, 24: 144–164.

Jonze, S. (Director) (1999). *Being John Malkovich* (film).

Kohut, H. (1971). *The Analysis of the Self*. London: Hogarth Press.

Kristeva, J. (1987). *Black Sun: Depression and Melancholia*, L. S. Roudiez (Trans.). New York: Columbia University Press.

Lindgren, A. (2002). *Most Beloved Sister*, E. K. Dyssegaard (Trans.). San Jose: R & R. Books.

McDougall, J. (1980). *Plea for a Measure of Abnormality*. New York: International Universities Press.

McDougall, J. (1995). *The Many Faces of Eros*. London: Free Association Books.

Olsson, H. (1990). *Edith Södergranin kirjeet* [Edith's letters], P. Saaritsa (Trans.). Helsinki: Otava.

Reenkola, E. (2006). *Intohimoinen nainen* (Female Desire). Helsinki: Gaudeamus Helsinki University Press.

Rieder, I., & Voigt, D. (2000). *Heimliches Begehren*. Wien – Munich: Deuticke.

Segal, H. (1957). Note on symbol formation. *International Journal of Psychoanalysis*, *38*: 391–397.

Södergran, E. (1984). *Complete Poems*, D. McDuff (Trans.). Newcastle: Bloodaxe Books.

Södergran, E. (1990). *The Poems by Edith Södergran*, G. Brown (Trans.), drawings by J. Griffiths. Penrhyndendraeth: Zena.

Södergran, E. (1992). *Love and Solitude. Selected Poems 1926–1923* (3rd edn), S. Katchadourian (Trans.). Seattle: Fjord Press.

Winnicott, D. W. (1971). *Playing and Reality*. London: Tavistock.

Young-Bruehl, E. (1988). *Anna Freud*. London: Macmillan.

Young-Bruehl, E. (1993). *Subject to Biography*. Cambridge, MA: Harvard University Press.

CHAPTER SEVEN

Conflicts around having two mothers: an interview study with a Finnish war child

Barbara Mattsson

Introduction

This study presents an interview with a Finnish woman who, as a child, was evacuated to Sweden during the Second World War and who did not permanently return to her homeland after the war.

During the war years of 1939–1945, about 80,000 Finnish children were evacuated to neighbouring countries, primarily Sweden.

Almost immediately after the war started in 1939, in the beginning on private initiative from Sweden came an invitation to Finland expressing a willingness to provide homes for Finnish children in order to protect them from the dangers of war. In Finland, these children were then, and still are, referred to as war children. The evacuation of children was carried out in accordance with terms specified by the Finnish government and took place for the most part by boat or train. The transport of children could take between two and six days. The groups were large, about 600 children per transport. There was usually one attendant per thirty children (Kaven, 2010). Upon arrival in Sweden, the children were required to spend a certain time in quarantine.

In the summer of 2007, ten Finnish war children who did not return to Finland on a permanent basis at the end of the war were interviewed by two Finnish, but Swedish-speaking, researchers. The interviews were unstructured and began with the open request, "Tell me about your life." The research interest was to explore how childhood experiences of wartime evacuation are reflected in adult memories. One of these interviews is presented here as a case study with a focus on the interviewee's inner conflict around having two mothers, her biological mother in Finland and her adopted mother in Sweden.

"Grounded theory" (Glaser, 1992, 1994), where the basic approach is to study the material, without ready-made hypotheses, was used as the primary method. At the same time, the preconception that the break-up of the family and the adjustment to a new family, a new culture and a new language would be associated with severe challenges cannot be disregarded. A little child's relation to its mother and separation from her are often characterized in terms of attachment, trauma and loss. A disruption in the early mother–child relationship can be considered to be the main causes of psychological disturbances and may appear immediately or later in life (Bowlby et al., 1939; Freud & Burlingham, 1943).

The interviewers read the transcribed interviews together repeatedly, at the same time trying to be unbiased and open to emerging themes and listening to the material with the third ear, that is, interpreting it in the light of clinical experience and through the knowledge of early infant–parent interaction.

Observations in the larger study

The stories collected in the larger interview study (of ten adult war children) had great individual variation. In the case presented here, we have applied the following themes generated in the larger study: conflict because of two pairs of parents, feelings of emptiness, rage, and signs of traumatic reactions. All participants had to relate to the fact that they had two sets of parents. Almost all of them had parental images with marked idealisations of one of the parental couples, most commonly the adoptive parents. Emptiness was expressed in various formulations such as "I am nothing", "I have no roots", "It's like a black hole". Rage was expressed directly or in hidden ways as projections or projective identification. The participants also showed obvious signs of traumatic reactions, for example, expressions of timelessness, indicating difficulties in maintaining a stable inner structure or mental space, disrupted thinking, and fragmented narratives with interruptions or memory blanks, various affective reactions, and also somatic expressions of affect, for example, coughing, stammering, and laughing.

By observing the interplay between the interviewer and the interviewee, an important methodological finding came to light, which was that transference and countertransference phenomena were in force and could also be used as sources of information in interviews.

All the interviewed individuals were members of a war child association and voluntarily participated in the study. All were well educated and professionally well established and had stable family bonds and relationships. With the exception of one seven-year-old, they were been between two and four years old when evacuated from Finland. Kirsti was one of them.

The interview

A short summary of Kirsti's background

Kirsti was born in 1938 in Helsinki and moved with her family to the countryside after the outbreak of the war. In the family there were six children, two of whom were younger than Kirsti. Her father served in the war. When she was two years old, she spent two months at a children's home, together with her siblings, because her mother was in the hospital. When Kirsti was almost four years old, it seems that the municipal physician urged Kirsti's mother to send her to Sweden since she was obviously undernourished. Sent off in 1942, she came to a childless foster family in a small town in the middle of Sweden. Two of her brothers were also later sent to Sweden, but to different places.

In 1946, Kirsti was sent back to her Finnish family in accordance with a regulation that applied to all Finnish war children. However, she remained in Finland only two months and then returned to Sweden, something she herself keenly desired. She protested against her stay in Finland by refusing to eat. Later on, Kirsti did well in school, took a university degree, married, and had two children.

Selected parts of Kirsti's life story

The interview took about two hours and was taped and transcribed. The order of the selected parts is the same as it was in the actual interview. Some words considered especially meaningful are italicised.

Interviewer:	Tell me about your life.
Kirsti:	Well [laughs], that won't be so easy. Where do you think I should begin?
Interviewer:	Just as it occurs to you.
(Silence.)	
Interviewer:	Hmm.
Kirsti:	Do you mean from the beginning or . . .
Interviewer:	I mean that it is completely up to you to decide.
Kirsti:	Oh, well.
Interviewer:	I'm inviting you . . .
Kirsti:	It might take a long time.
Interviewer:	Well, we have some time.
Kirsti:	We have some time—OK. Then I'll start from the beginning, when I was born.
Interviewer:	That's absolutely OK.
Kirsti:	I was born in Helsinki and in 1942—No, what am I saying? (laughs). I have no idea where I am, in 1938 . . . yes, exactly. I came to Sweden in 1942 and . . .
Interviewer:	How nice. You can talk about two births.

She said that she was born when she came to Sweden. The time perspective disappeared. The interviewer supported her so that the mix-up would not feel too difficult. After this, Kirsti became more precise, providing many details. Was it important for her to show that she was well orientated?

Kirsti:	Well . . . I have almost always talked about that because when I came to Sweden in 1942 the passage to Sweden was hard work, because it was an incredibly cold winter that

January. The boat with the war children on board got stuck in the ice in the Gulf of Finland, so there was talk of helicopter transportation to take food and water down to the boat, but the problem solved itself, eventually. Then we arrived in Stockholm. Those days were especially dramatic, but we had to spend time in Stockholm in the hospital for [medical] examinations. Only after that did I go on to Västerås, where it had been decided that I should go, and my Swedish mother came to pick me up at the hospital for infectious diseases and the only memory I have from the hospital is the stone step on the stairs. I previously had very many memories of the trip and my life in Finland, although I was so young when I left; I was only three years old. I was three when I travelled to Sweden and I was four when I arrived, so I had my [fourth] birthday there.

Kirsti immediately took over the description of the two births. When she talked about the hardships of the passage, she had the perspective of an adult, describing details she could not have known about when it all happened. When she described the stairs, she focuses on a detail, thus diverting her attention from overwhelming feelings. Focusing on a detail indicates a link to trauma (Kaplan, 2006).

Interviewer: You had your birthday.

Kirsti: Well, sometimes I say it this way: sometimes I'm three and sometimes I'm four, but then anyway when I talk about my birthday the picture in my mind is when my mother had picked me up and it was terribly cold; it was cold in Sweden then, too; it was minus 30–40 degrees centigrade. They were those cold wartime winters, so she swept me up in a blanket, I was very small; I was already four but I was only about 88 cm tall, so I was like a little two-year-old. My mother had sewn clothes for me that should have been for a four-year old, everything was 20 cm too big, but that special feeling when my foster mother swept me up in the blanket and we went in a taxi or a car home then I used to talk about *my second birth* for it was such a fantastic feeling, *I think* that now I came to people who were *incredibly good-hearted and fine* and *I think* I felt it through the blanket—yes, it felt like that—not only was it . . . it [stammering] warm and comfy and that someone was holding me, but it was as if something pulled right through me. And at the same time I felt enormously secure, there was a person then who after all those weeks took care of me, and that's why I talk about my second birth [laughs] when *I'm sitting* there in the blanket *coming home* to Sweden.

The present tense (timelessness) suggests an activated trauma during the interview itself. It might also be that she was afraid, even though she herself said something altogether different. It is also possible that after all her trials during the journey Kirsti immediately clung to the person who took care of her and only her. Here, again, we see an adult perspective in her narrative, for example, when she said that she felt she had come to good-hearted people. It is characteristic of her way of talking that at first she hesitates about some detail but then decides that this was exactly the way it was.

Interviewer: You can still feel this—the feeling you had?

Kirsti brought the feeling into the present moment and the interviewer picked it up.

Kirsti: Yes, I can recognise it. I recognise the blanket. It was in the 1940s. It was probably a grey [extra] blanket that was perhaps stored in a box? It was so cold—that sort of dark grey blanket and then there were grey stripes in a lighter grey; I remember that.

She jumped from the present affect to a concrete object (trauma linking). She described the blanket, but not her mother or the house she had come to, and neither did she introduce her Swedish family.

Kirsti: And so I also remember, or have some memory pictures in my mind, when we arrived there and I felt an enormous sense of trust right away and, you know, I also remember how my Swedish mamma got a meal ready, I mean she was the one who got the instructions. They told the Swedish people to take care of us children so that we didn't get . . . I mean we were undernourished with swollen stomachs. I was in really bad shape, but not so sick that I needed to be in the hospital. They weren't supposed to give us anything

sweet and that was, you know, very important. I remember
the first meal my mamma cooked. I thought it was what they
called Lapland porridge, I think it was probably only rye
flakes or something like that and not sweet, that porridge,
and then there was a little milk, *maybe*, and then, to top it off,
there was a little lingonberry jam, and I thought it was so
good, it was so fantastic. Or this is just a mental picture of
that food, because I knew that my mamma had to be very
careful—the stomachs [of people like me] were so delicate,
but also this—you sat down to eat, and consequently I had a
lot of trust in my mamma. And I remember the plates, we
had them later as well, this whole Gustavsberg . . . [China
set].

The food tasted good. Here, her trust seems to be a memory of an
experience. She emphasised her Swedish mother's caring ways. She
also noted the china set that she ate from.

Kirsti: I was fearful when a stranger came in. This was because the
             environment was new; people spoke Swedish that I didn't
             understand, and I know, well, partly . . . remember that. But
             then, also, it probably was my mamma who told the story,
             and it was perhaps a week or so later when I was sitting at
             the table having my food and sat like that with the spoon,
             and when my mamma's friend *comes in* and *greets* us, and *I
             do not move for twenty minutes* because this *is*, this *is* typical of
             Finnish war children, something you *read* about in the news-
             paper. "They were, of course, nice, docile as they were . . ."
             [In truth] we were more or less panic-stricken in some way
             in many situations (cough). I was apathetic, in some way, I
             think, this was an effect of . . . When just a few minutes
             before I had been laughing and been lively with my mamma,
             and then curious people knocked on the door, and mamma
             and papa didn't have any children, and if a neighbour got a
             child everybody just stared, but *I do not move* until she had
             left. Of course, this [behaviour] passed, it's just a reaction I
             remember . . .

Here, Kirsti told us that she was panic-stricken and, at the same
time, apathetic in the face of the unexpected and unknown. Being
paralysed is a powerful trauma indicator, a frozen reaction (Krystal,
1978). In the interview, the affect was somatised (cough). Kirsti said

that the frozen reaction in the presence of strangers gradually passed; later, her anxiety found expression in other ways. She overcame her frozen reactions, but would instead run away when strangers arrived.

Kirsti talked a long time about her shyness and talked about her language difficulties. She did not know Swedish from earlier times, although her biological father spoke Swedish. Not knowing the language spoken by those with whom one lives and being unable to understand and make oneself understood are conditions we regard as traumatic.

Kirsti gradually turned to thoughts of her life in Finland.

> Kirsti: Well, it was like this. On the one hand *I lived in Helsinki* and I *imagine* that when things were at their worst in 1940 we moved out to the countryside outside, to Porvoo, since my father was Finnish-Swedish and my mother was from Karelia, and it was from there (Porvoo) *I then moved to Sweden* . . . I was three that winter or . . . that winter I would be four. I remember rather many pictures from that [time], particularly I remember the late summer before, when I was three and a half; maybe . . . because it was such a positive memory: it is summer and we were six siblings, so I had two brothers or three—no, wait, four brothers and a sister and then had two brothers who were smaller and then there was one who was a baby then, and it is just this that I remember from the summer; the sun *is* shining and I liked the walk and *I'm sitting* on *Äiti's* [Finnish for *mother's*] lap and this has, like, stuck in my mind, and I have gradually understood now, later on, why it has stuck: it was of course because of, the fact that, besides, she [mother] had a brother who was two years younger than I, he was probably one and a half or perhaps two, and in addition a [my] baby brother who natu-rally took up her attention and time, and then there was me, who was allowed to follow along on that walk. It was only me, that is, there weren't any siblings with us, but there was me.

She began the narrative about her Finnish family with a possible construction of her early life, a construction she did not seem to be completely sure of. She described herself as separate from her family: she was not moved to Sweden; she was the one who moved. She spoke as if the initiative had been hers and that she had control over what happened. In her mind, is she the one responsible for her being sent to Sweden?

She told how she sat on *Äiti's* lap. *Äiti* and she were the central figures in this picture and the siblings were her competitors.

Interviewer: You and your mother . . .

Kirsti: Yes. It was just *Äiti*, I make a distinction between *Äiti*, *Äiti* in Finland, and . . . my mamma in Sweden; you know this is a good way to make a distinction . . .

Interviewer: Yes.

Kirsti: . . . so that . . . that image in my memory in which the sun is shining and we have picked flowers, and then I don't remember much more until the winter and then partly a picture of my father who was home on leave on Christmas Eve, [in that image] . . . I, like, only *see* how he *sits* down and *lights* the candles on the Christmas tree, I remember that and I remember the Christmas tree. I don't know if it was a Finnish tradition to hang apples on the Christmas tree, maybe it's a mistake, maybe there was an apple on the table . . . Anyway I remember that there was an apple.

The memory of traditions in the home told us that she connected to good memories that she may possibly be able to pass on (see Kaplan, 2006, 2008). There was a tentative, reflective mood at this point in Kirsti's story. After this, her father disappeared from the narrative.

Interviewer: It was certainly very worthwhile to have the apples, those winter apples.

Kirsti: Yes, they certainly were winter apples. That's very likely, because they were so heavy, they were hanging on the tree . . . Then I also remember a time before that, maybe it was in the autumn; we were playing, there wasn't much to play with . . . *Äiti* was cleaning and she of course had rag rugs, and they were rolled up and taken out and beaten, or were already cleaned and had been taken in, and I played with that rag rug; maybe I was inspired by her [*Äiti*], for she was feeding my little baby brother, so that *I'm sitting* there with that rag rug in my arms, and there wasn't so much food, she had made pancakes. I remember that there were pancakes or maybe those small pancakes and I *feed* the rug with the small pancakes [laughs], stuck the food into one end, yes, I remember that and then I remember that when I *play* as I did then, then those pancakes had got sticky, and I was told not to feed the rug with pancakes. But then also, this was probably just before I was going to travel to Sweden and so we were out playing and it was the same thing there—there was a lot of snow and it was cold, yards high, so that we had dug out tunnels in the snow—I was so little then, so high [shows], and you could draw in the new snow, so then and there [in the snow] I drew plates, for my sister and myself, so you could sit as if you were at table. And I also remember the snow cave that perhaps the boys had made and where they locked me in; it wasn't any fun, I remember.

Kirsti took over the interviewer's thoughts of winter apples and *knew* that they were hanging on the tree. She gave a vivid picture of the interior of her Finnish home; Kirsti was sitting on the floor to eat, Äiti had the little brother in her arms. Why was she playing with the food? Kirsti was said to be undernourished. She was also feeding "a baby"/the rug, as mother did with the baby brother. Was this an illustration of her eating difficulties? It can also be seen as an imitative act to deny her sense of exclusion from Äiti.

She had a tendency to describe herself and exclude others, in this case her sister. The game with the plates was not at first described as a game they played together. Neither did the interview become a mutual "game". Kirsti could recall unpleasant experiences, but most of the things she remembered and told about her relationships were sunny memories. Again, it can be noted that parts of the story were told in the present tense.

Kirsti: . . . I remember the boat trip but not the leave taking [from Äiti], I don't remember when Äiti left me and I think that's something, I think that's the way it was, that there I must have felt some kind of, well I don't know, disappointment and so abandoned by, I had no one else, I mean in perspective, I had my beloved mother in Sweden but then I had no one else but Äiti, and Papa had been in the war since 1939, so then I had Äiti and then I was sent away, since I don't remember this at all . . .

> I remember the boat trip, I remember the playmates on the boat, I remember that there were a brother and sister that I wished I could have met again some time, I thought they were so adorable, he was, the boy, was probably about my age, maybe five years old. He was wearing a red shirt and he had a little sister, who had curly brown hair and was maybe two years old. And I have a really easy time remembering the material that clothes are made of, how they look—what someone is wearing—and I remember exactly the checked skirt she was wearing or the dress . . .

Her narrative activated the traumatic separation from *Äiti*. This was one of the few events she did not claim to remember. But she remembered the pattern in the material of the girl's skirt.

Kirsti: I think also that there was, I don't know, I think that perhaps it was some kind of, well I thought of it as some kind of disappointment, for I don't really know what my attitude towards her was when I came to Sweden, so consequently all the time I was thinking about this [I asked myself], was it like this? *I belong*, of course, to those who were lucky: there was communication between Finland and Sweden, between parents, I mean. My *Äiti* wrote, and it was translated, the librarian in Västerås translated all the letters. Of course, they were clipped by the censors, if someone had written something unsuitable about the war. Of course there was censorship but there was communication, and they immediately sent photographs of . . . of [stammering]—*Äiti* had gone to a photographer after I left, and *my mamma always put out the photo Äiti sent on the bureau.* So, I had it and at the same time felt that I was not part of it (laughs); they were my other siblings, so I knew all the time, I knew from the picture what she and my siblings looked like, and such, but—but [stammering] at the same time I think I also knew that when you are little you can sense a conflict when you love two people.

Something happened to Kirsti's picture of *Äiti*. Kirsti wondered what she felt. She recalled her traumatic memories and tried to talk about them. This led to reflection. Her narrative also included later constructions relating to the exchange of letters and the censorship; it was not merely a child's perspective. Kirsti had a tendency to laugh when the affects were activated. "Mamma always put out the photograph on the bureau," said Kirsti. But who took it down?

She said that she had a conflict when she loved two people. She put the conflict in words. However, she was perhaps not always so conscious about this conflict. Her happiness in Sweden, with her mother, was seriously threatened.

> *Kirsti*:   I had terrible anxiety when I came to Sweden, when I was little, I mean. Well, but . . . but [stammering] . . . but all this about catastrophes, it's just about things that are connected to mamma. If my [Swedish] father had died I would have been extremely sorry but, if I were to know that mamma should die then I wouldn't have managed at all. I mean my experience tells me that I would not have been able to handle it. But then just that . . . that [stammering] which I understand were tricks for mastering my anxiety—probably started very early after I arrived, because [sometimes later] my father might say something like that I was so orderly, because I folded up my clothes so neatly . . . That was, of course, something positive that he could say to my mamma: "she is so orderly, she folds her clothes so neatly, she lays them on the chair." Afterwards I have realised that even there, for I remember that I busied myself with such things, this was a way to get the upper hand over chaos [and] that you could perhaps repeat things or you could put away things very nicely and so.

> *Interviewer*:   Things in order?

> *Kirsti*:   I always *see* catastrophe ahead. It must be connected to the fact that I came as a war child.

> *Interviewer*:   This farewell . . .?

> *Kirsti*:   Yes, partly. But also this, I *think* that the worst had happened. It is the same kind of feeling that I have toward things [that are good], the feeling that I must destroy them. I do not do it but I *feel* that way . . . I must not feel this joy and happiness, so then I have to destroy it. And then I think, then that she [mamma] will die. And I had a lot of those anxiety tics.

> When I was little I had an extremely strong fear of death and of course that also has a connection [with what hap-

pened], because that was the first summer, the second summer, I was five years old, when mamma picked peonies; they *are* so beautiful and *have* such a lovely scent. They were in a vase on the table and the whole time I had to turn around and look at the peonies, for I knew that they were the last I would see since I was convinced that *I'll die* tonight and that was overwhelming: [It wasn't only mamma who would die], I would also die, and just these very peonies would be lost to me. Now I have peonies in the garden at our country home that are wonderful, and I don't think about this any more, but earlier they were associated with death . . . [In those times] I had to turn around and look at the peonies one last time and then creep down [in bed?], and it was also like this, you know, when you have to repeat things several times, I had to look one more time at the peonies because *this is the last time* I'll see them, and then, well, there was so much more like that . . . I remember myself, how I like stared or opened my eyes wide, and maybe mamma said, "Don't do that with your eyes, it might not be good for them", after which I thought that I would be blind. So that was also a kind of fright, that I would be blind, so that I had to . . . it could never be completely dark, it mustn't be so now either. If it's pitch dark I jump out of bed and believe I'm blind.

Someone would die, mamma or herself. Was she "blind" when she was separated from *Äiti* and lost contact with her?

Kirsti: I know now, of course, that I could very easily [still] fall into things I did in childhood: you threw the ball, repeated it fifty-eleven times because *otherwise mamma dies*, and then you were completely worn out, that's the way it often was when I was doing something. It was a number thing, four times and four times and still there could be something negative, and if I did it three times there was one time left, then mamma might say "don't do that", maybe she was annoyed with me, perhaps it was something I shouldn't be doing, and then I panicked because why should she stop me now when I had just one time left . . .

Negative as well as positive feelings were forbidden and dangerous and had to be mastered.

Kirsti emphasised that she had been well taken care of in Sweden. An example of this was how she thought of her first meals in Sweden; she sat at a table and was the object of mamma's care. She considered herself the centre of her new family. It can be assumed that such a self-image was also supported by the idea that she could steer or control the adults' decisions, either magically, as in the anxious experiences and memories just presented, or, more realistically, for example, when she wished and was allowed to travel back to Sweden and where her food protest played some role. She was seriously undernourished when she came back to Sweden.

Kirsti recalled her time as a university student. She noted at a later point that she, even as an adult, could suddenly start to run and at the same time shout inside herself, "No—no!"

Kirsti:	Well, then there was the anxiety during my time as a student in another town. I was depressed for a while and went to the doctor.
Interviwer:	This was, of course, an enormous separation, for a young adult or teenager.
Kirsti:	So that . . .
Inerviewer:	Many young people regard this period as challenging.
Kirsti:	I didn't think it was, *I know*: they called it some kind of inner depression that was caused by some thing or other! But it was probably a concurrence of concurrence [repetition] of various factors, I think.

This is an example of how Kirsti defended herself against the interviewer's thoughts about separation anxiety. She was not ready to listen. She did not do the interview together with the interviewer or take note of what she herself did not completely understand. As Kirsti wanted to be in command of her own life, it was difficult for her to listen to others.

When Kirsti's *Äiti* visited Sweden when she had her confirmation, Kirsti avoided her, perhaps as she avoided the interviewer. She declared that she was ashamed of her *Äiti*, who wanted to sing Finnish songs. She wondered why it was easier to associate with *Äiti* in Finland when her [Swedish] mamma was not present.

Discussion

Here, Kirsti's interview will be discussed via the grounded theory themes: the interviewer's countertransference, Kirsti's hidden reactions to feelings of emptiness and rage and manifestations of trauma, and, finally, with regard to her conflict of having two mothers.

Countertransference

In Kirsti's narrative, it often seemed as if no dialogue with the interviewer would develop. Recurrently, she either did not hear the interviewer's questions or responded to them by talking over the top of the interviewer. Sometimes, the interviewer was not allowed to finish speaking; there was an interruption in communication. The interviewer recalled that early in the interview she noted Kirsti's sensitivity. She also had the feeling that she was holding her breath and could not speak spontaneously and, therefore, became cautious when she felt controlled. There are two messages with regard to the most manifest transference–countertransference dynamic: in Kirsti's world, one does not do things together and control is important. With these postures, which were strongly felt by the interviewer, Kirsti conveyed something of her frozen reactions to the interviewer.

McDougall (among many others) has emphasised that it is particularly important to listen to countertransference when engaged in so-called primitive communication (McDougall, 1979). She describes how a person can use his speech as an action when catastrophic events have made it impossible to keep together or to process emotional experiences. The speech then contains a message that has not been processed on a verbal level and, therefore, can only be fully listened to or registered by reflecting on the countertransference. Instead of feeling and remembering, the patient needs to get the therapist to feel and experience.

Feelings of emptiness

Kirsti was chosen as a contrast to those other children of war whom we have studied, who often talked openly about their feelings of emptiness. Kirsti's narrative was different, and in parts of the interview she supplied us with powerful images of her early childhood.

On other occasions, she told, also in rich detail, about things that she herself could not possibly have remembered or known about at the time to which she was referring. She then adopted an adult perspective, relating things she did not remember directly, and the narrative took on a defensive character. She did not want to be a person who did not know. Ignorance and the subsequent helplessness seemed to be humiliating and painful to her. She had developed strong defences against loneliness and helplessness.

Many psychoanalysts use the concept of emptiness, emptiness experiences, and black holes in their description of narcissistic traits, early disturbances, autistic reactions, and deep depressions. Severe psychic trauma always causes a lasting narcissistic wound. The traumatised person may further feel that the inner object's protective function has failed and that what is meaningful in his/her existence has fallen apart. This might create a feeling of inner loneliness and great helplessness. Traumatic experiences can destroy the protection that had previously been formed by empathetic, internalised, primary objects (Böhm & Kaplan, 2011; Garland, 1998; Gerzi, 2005).

Rage

Thoughts of hidden disappointment and rage were aroused by Kirsti's narratives about her compulsive actions as a child (Winnicott, 1990). Her way of dealing with affects was to keep unmanageable emotional experiences outside the self and outside the sphere of her interactions with those who were close to her. She struggled with her dread of becoming blind or dying, and above all with her fear that her mother might die. She also had difficulties in putting into words disappointment or anger: she expressed mostly good memories of her relation to others.

Untreated or unconscious anger can be expressed by vengeful actions or thoughts of revenge (Kaplan, 2008). Such fantasies can tell us about affects that the subject is not capable of reflecting upon. In the background, there may be early feelings of shame. Was it a vengeful act when Kirsti abandoned *Äiti*?

Traumatic reactions

In the selection of interview passages for the present account, reactions that were considered to be traumatic have been pointed out.

Memories that emerged during the course of the narrative activated painful affects. However, Kirsti usually managed to recount and reflect on these memories. When she agreed to tell her story, she dared to take the risk of being emotionally affected. She was, thus, able to convert in a creative way some of her traumatic memories into something vital in the present. She also referred to details: china, interior decoration, songs, and poems. That is, Kirsti actively worked through aspects of her trauma and tried to find a space for a normal life and an existence in the present (Kaplan, 2008). There was a great deal of flexibility in Kirsti's affective reactions. In these areas, her trauma did not prevent psychic work.

It is possible to discern more severe effects of her trauma in her easily aroused anxiety and in her thoughts of catastrophes, as well as in the ready-made scenario she stuck to during the interview. The traumatised person is on the lookout for a repetition of the trauma. When Kirsti was on guard against questions, this might be an avoidance of traumatic affect reactions that might lead to a repetition of the trauma. In the interview, she repeatedly felt acutely threatened, which could be noted through the timelessness in her narrative and her efforts to maintain control. Her good memory sense of details, which obviously already existed before her evacuation to Sweden, can be seen as a special talent, but it may also have served defensive needs. When she became attached to a single neutral detail, such as the stone of the steps, the pattern in the girl's dress, and the blanket she was wrapped in, this was her way of diverting attention from her own psychic inner state.

Traumatisation can also be perceived in her frozen reactions in surprising situations. Krystal (1978) makes a distinction between infantile trauma and adult trauma. Infantile trauma can be compared to "deadly fear" (mortal fright), while the adult has a self-observing ego that seldom is completely put out of play. Children's reactions to trauma depend on their developmental stage and the defences that are available. The effects of the trauma activate the narcissistic defences (Gertzi, 2005). After the evacuation, Kirsti had to protect her narcissistic vulnerability from traumatic experiences with early defences such as denial and projection. Traumatic events in childhood may also release intractable aggression that brings with it a fear of losing control over aggressive wishes and fear of magically causing destruction (Krystal, 1978).

It seems as if Kirsti was especially sensitive about not knowing and not understanding. Not knowing and not understanding lead to help-lessness. In the interview, she tended to immediately pick up some-thing the interviewer said and turn it into her own truth (her second birthday, the winter apples). This is something one might call her "closed system" (Novick & Novick, 2011), where she does not want to be dependent on another person, for example, not on the interviewer's understanding either. The Novicks distinguish between locked, omnipotent, and sadomasochistic ways to meet life, which allow little opportunity for development, and the opposite, where one strives for a change of the self. Kirsti's feeling that she must destroy what is good can be seen as a manifestation of a closed system that includes obsta-cles to being helped. The Novicks emphasise that a closed system may form an effective defence against the experience of helplessness and, therefore, that it can be difficult to refrain from the locked position.

Compulsive features may also occur as a thin membrane between the present and underlying, threatening experiences of emptiness and isolation (Tustin, 1986).

Two pairs of parents

That both mothers were the pervading themes in the interview reflects what could be called the eternal conflict of Finnish war children. Kirsti's relation to her adopted mother seemed to be characterised by idealisation ("my beloved mother"). She was not described as an inde-pendent person in her own right. *Äiti*, on the other hand, was des-cribed more like a living person whom Kirsti kept at a distance. Even though she could reflect from time to time upon her conflict in rela-tion to *Äiti*, Kirsti's tendency to dissociate was also discernible in her attitude to the interviewer, whose contributions were repeatedly inter-rupted and dismissed or taken over.

Many war children reported how shameful it was to be the one sent away. Kirsti seemed to experience shame and expressed it in projective ways. When *Äiti* visited Sweden at her confirmation, Kirsti avoided her. She said that she was ashamed of her *Äiti*, who wanted to sing Finnish songs. Kirsti turned her back on her "old" mother. However, she acknowledged that she had a tendency to destroy what was good: she had some reconciliation with, and understanding of, *Äiti* in adulthood.

Fathers were glimpsed only in the periphery in the interview. A missed father might be a factor that goes together with feelings of emptiness and regressive and destructive tendencies.

She said that she felt fortunate to be the only child in her Swedish family. When her Swedish papa said that he was sorry that she did not have any siblings in her Swedish family, she most decidedly did not agree with him.

Kirsti's solution to the problem of two sets of parents was that she chose her mother in Sweden as number one in her life, but she maintained her contact with her *Äiti*. However, the person she described and talked about the most in her interview was *Äiti*. In reality, Kirsti had forgotten the Finnish language and could never again speak to her *Äiti* without a translator.

Different models of interpretation

It is possible to try to understand Kirsti partly by reflecting over her earlier life in Finland and partly by trying to understand the effects of the evacuation.

"Then I moved to Sweden" suggests that Kirsti had a notion that she could decide over her own life and which, in her mind, made her guilty for the separation from *Äiti*: had she abandoned *Äiti*? Was this the source of her various compulsive actions? When she came to Sweden, she immediately took on denial as a central defence. She tried to cope with the inconceivable by means of different actions. In order to maintain a living psyche, she attached herself quickly and defensively to her Swedish mother; "the porridge was so good". But this still did not protect her sufficiently; when a stranger came in, she became paralysed, revealing how dangerous and frightening her world had become.

Waddell (1998), among many others, describes the way babies during the earliest stages of their development take charge of their mother by looking at her. If the child does not find mother's affirming glance, it is a catastrophe for the child. The dawning psyche of the child is then threatened with annihilation anxiety, that is to say, psychic death. Is it possible that Kristi's fear of death and blindness was a return to that earlier state of "not seeing mother"?

The fear that someone is going to die has its origin in unconscious aggression. First, this aggression strikes a blow at the image of the mother and can later be transferred to a person that is present. Also, compulsive actions tell of unconscious aggression.

If the mother has not been able to function as a containing figure, there will be far-reaching consequences. The child can then attach herself to objects, sounds, or her own body in order to compensate for the deficiency. Under such circumstances, the outer world becomes the important one and the inner world is not developed (Tustin, 1986; Waddell, 1998). Kirsti's amazing early memories and exact images indicate a disposition to attach herself to concrete objects.

Sandler and Sandler (1998) described how insecure psychic structures might lead a person to drop from consciousness what is disturbing and unknown and turn to what is certain and familiar. The unknown may be interpreted as catastrophic, albeit at a distance. If a person has not developed his or her own structures that will carry through separation and disappointments, he or she might cling to idealised figures in the external word. Persons with insecure psychic structures might also, as adults, have a need to drop what is disturbing and unknown in their surroundings and turn to what is certain and familiar. Kirsti told us only good memories about her relations to others.

Most of the interviewees said that they did not have any memory of the journey to Sweden, or of their stay in quarantine. Kirsti said that she had many memories from the trip, making her unique in our group of war children. It seems especially unique because the whole evacuation to Sweden, the boat or train trip and the time in quarantine, can be regarded as one long stretch of events that for such young children would mean a period of being unable to understand their experiences as they were torn away from the contexts that were familiar to them (family, surroundings, and language).

Little children cannot understand different courses of events in their lives if they do not have an adult close to them who can help them interpret what is going on (Bion, 1962; Varvin, 2010). Kirsti did remember events from the evacuation, as specific concrete details, but she did not remember how she felt.

The significance of lack of containing can be seen in an earlier study with focus on the whole interview material (Mattsson & Maliniemi-Piispanen, 2013). This lack had an influence on the capacity to experience mourning and loss and, therewith, on the development on thinking as well (Bion, 1962). The evacuation also affected the adult war children's capacity to experience grief and losses and left a lasting imprint on their capacity to reflect on their own lives.

The interview with Kirsti had certain recurring themes. There were, for example, several instances in which traumatic manifestations were present and aroused during the interview. She tried to avoid the significance of her inability to remember or to understand and when she focused on things she was uncertain about, it seems clear that strong defences were mobilised against her helplessness. Her solution was various forms of control. These might have been remaining vestiges of previous overpowering events in her life, but, above all, they were meaningful reactions in the present.

Kirsti's central communication patterns were attempts to hold together childhood experiences that were split at an early age. She tried to defend herself in various ways against the feeling of not knowing, helplessness, and psychic conflict. It is probably an element in the lives of all children who were evacuated when they were small children that reflects the Finnish war child's exposed situation. Kirsti's reactions reveal something that concerns all the interviewed war children: reactions to losses that lead to an inner void and contribute to vulnerability in facing later disappointments and frustrations. Such experiences are difficult to handle when there is no known, distinct, legitimate aim, or an object for the anger and the ambivalence.

References

Bion, W. (1962). *Learning from Experience*. London: Heinemann.

Böhm, T., & Kaplan, S. (2011). *Revenge. On the Dynamics of a Frightening Urge and its Taming*. London: Karnac.

Bowlby, J., Miller, E., & Winnicott, D. W. (1939). Letter: Evacuation of small children. In: C. Garland (Ed.), (1998). *Understanding Trauma*. London: Karnac.

Freud, A., & Burlingham, D. (1943). *War and Children*. New York: Medical War Books.

Garland, C. (Ed.) (1998). *Understanding Trauma. A Psychoanalytic Approach*. London: Karnac.

Gertzi, S. (2005). Trauma, narcissism and the two attractors of trauma. *International Journal of Psychoanalysis*, 86: 1033–1050.

Glaser, B. (1992). *Basics of Grounded Theory Analysis*. Mill Valley, CA: Sociology Press.

Glaser, B. (1994). *More Grounded Theory: A Reader.* Mill Valley, CA: Sociology Press.

Kaplan, S. (2006). Children in genocide. Extreme traumatisation and the affect propeller. *International Journal of Psychoanalysis, 87*: 725–746.

Kaplan, S. (2008). *Children in Genocide. Extreme Traumatization and Affect Regulation.* London: International Psychoanalysis Library.

Kaven, P. (2010). *Humanitaarisuuden varjossa. Poliittiset tekijät lastensiirroissa Ruotsiin sotiemme aikana ja niiden jälkeen* [In the shadow of humanitarianism. Political factors in child evacuation to Sweden during our wars and later]. PhD thesis in History, Helsinki University.

Krystal, M. D. (1978). Trauma and affects. *Psychoanalytic Study of the Child, 33*: 81–112.

McDougall, J. (1979). Primitive communication and the use of countertransference. *Contemporary Psychoanalysis, 14*: 173–209.

Mattsson, B., & Maliniemi-Piispanen, S. (2013). Thinking about the unknown. An interview study of Finnish war children. *Trauma and Memory, 1*: 52–71.

Novick, J., & Novick, K. K. (2010). Sadomasochistic obstacles to the developmental transition from adolescence to adulthood: the closed system of self-regulation. Unpublished lecture in Helsinki.

Sandler, J., & Sandler, A.-M. (1998). *Internal Objects Revisited.* London: Karnac.

Tustin, F. (1986). *Autistic Barriers in Neurotic Patients.* London: Karnac.

Varvin, S. (2010). The stranger and the strange: psychoanalytic reflections on meeting otherness. Paper presented to the XXII Nordic Psychoanalytic Congress. Helsinki, 5–8 August.

Waddell, M. (1998). *Inside Lives: Psychoanalysis and the Growth of the Personality.* London: Karnac.

Winnicott, D. (1990). *The Maturational Processes and the Facilitating Environment.* London: Karnac.

CHAPTER EIGHT

On the psychology of love

Esa Roos

Introduction

C an anyone say one what makes love happy or unhappy? In spite of the essentially subjective nature of the question, it is important to examine what factors lead to disappointment and failure of love and what factors lead to the hoped-for results, that is, to a happy union of individuals as well as a cohesive society. Why is love so central to our existence? Because it is a strong motivational force in life and a central interest for humanity. It is an extremely communicative state, a force for development, and a motivating and creative drive of human nature and culture. Love and happiness are not simply psychoanalytic terms. Both are well-known mental states, as well as hate and dream. Certain things are indispensable to happiness, such as food, health, work, parenthood, respect, and love. In being in love, we hope to find our happiness. Pascal Bruckner (2012) says that the modern family is centred on the happiness of its members (p. 130). According to him, "we love as much as human beings can love, that is, imperfectly" (p. 219).

It is also said that lovers are fools, that love is a temporary mental disturbance. When in love, one's whole world seems to be changed;

everything is upside down, out of the usual order. In the case of a happy outcome, life becomes more alive, hopeful, and meaningful. Fortune is within one's grasp, the future opens up, full of possibilities. Everything seems to be self-evident, easy, and paradise-like. According to Stendhal (1822, p. 228), the moment one begins to take interest in a person, one no longer sees him or her as they really are, but as it suits one to see them; one sees flattering illusions. In an unhappy case of love, life is filled with pain and misery, without meaning and hope. The important, longed-for experience is out of reach.

You cannot order anybody to love. According to Aristotle (1963) love is the basic condition for any kind of virtue (p. 291). What we love is valuable to us. Love as a source of joy and delight is, in the first instance, a value in itself. In our field, the love of truth and care for the other are similarly valued. In erotic life, we see many examples where the other person's value is only instrumental (pornography, incest, paedophilia, rape, etc.). Pentti Ikonen (2004) wrote, "Love reveals the intrinsic value of the object of love to us . . . What destroys or hinders our love, destroys and hinders the possibility of intrinsic values becoming revealed to us" (pp. 222–223).

Is there anything that can explain love? Martin Bergmann (1980) suggests that falling in love and staying in love are two separate phenomena, since in falling in love, only dim memories of a symbiotic phase are essential. In contrast, to maintain a love relationship requires considerable maturity. Bergmann's focus is on the refinding of the elements of the symbiotic phase. He states that the ego's first task is to observe the real qualities of the love object and evaluate the prognosis of this "lovely disease" (p. 73). According to Freud (1930a) "happiness, in the reduced sense in which we recognize it as possible, is a problem of the economics of the individual's libido" (p. 83). He also had serious doubts about the value of civilisation as a means to happiness (p. 89). About the death instinct, in contrast to Eros, he wrote, "The other of the two 'Heavenly Powers', eternal Eros will make an effort to assert himself in the struggle with his equally immortal adversary. But who can foresee with what success and with what result?" (p. 145).

Further theoretical perspectives on love

Is there a place for love in Freud's theory?

There is a widely held opinion that Freud had little to say about love and that he equated love with sexuality. *Both are mistaken.* Freud wrote on love over 130 times and planned to publish a book on it (Hitschmann, 1952). He contributed more to the understanding of love than anyone after Plato (see Bergmann, 1982). Freud distinguished at least three distinct types of love: anaclitic, narcissistic, and genital. In *Civilization and its Discontents* (1930a) he outlines the purpose of human life according to the pleasure–displeasure principle as the search for happiness and the avoidance of suffering.

It is a fact that pleasure exists and rules the beginning of any kind of love relation. Freud argues that civilisation fails to bring the happiness we expect from it, and without love man cannot survive. Every man must find for himself the object of love to whom he can direct his need for affectionate attachment and for binding his sensual and sexual passion.

In the psychoanalytic theory of development, the relationship between object love and sexual drives has always been a puzzle in the psychoanalytic theory of development (see Widlöcher, 2002). André Green (1995) and, recently, Peter Fonagy (2008) have noticed that there is an apparent decline of psychoanalytic interest in psychosexuality, which might be related to the criticism of drive theory and an increasing popularity of object relations theories.

Freud (1926d) discussed the biological factor of the "long period of time during which the young of the human species is in a condition of helplessness and dependence". This factor "establishes the earliest situations of danger and creates the need to be loved which will accompany the child through the rest of its life" (pp. 154–155). In 1905, when he published his ideas on infantile sexuality, he stated, "The prototype of every love relationship is the child sucking at his mother's breast. The finding of the love object is in fact a refinding" (Freud, 1905d, p. 222). I think that this means simply that you want to experience the familiar happiness and delight in re-meeting your love object again and again. The most popular play of all children is the peekaboo game (or fort-da, which was the name of the game Freud used in *Beyond the Pleasure Principle*, 1920g). But, interestingly enough, Bergmann (1988) argues that the refinding process goes much deeper than Freud discussed:

> If love is to be fulfilling, every important object in childhood must in some way be represented. When one of these objects has been

excluded through repression, love is experienced as incomplete, then one needs more than one love object at the same time or in succession. From the point of view of the ego, love represents a triumph of the integrative function over the needs of the id for separate and conflict-laden refindings of the many love objects of childhood. (pp. 670–671)

Bergmann points out the connection between refinding and integration. He acknowledges this insight as homage to Shakespeare:

> Thy bosom is endeared with all hearts,
> Which I by lacking have supposed dead,
> And there reigns love and all love's loving parts,
> And all those friends which I thought buried.
> How many a holy and obsequious tear
> Hath dear religious love stol'n from mine eye
> As interest of the dead, which now appear
> But things removed that hidden in thee lie!
> Thou art the grave where buried love doth live,
> Hung with the trophies of my lovers gone,
> Who all their parts of me to thee did give;
> That due of many now is thine alone,
> Their images I lov'd I view in thee,
> And thou, all they, hast all the all of me.
>   (Shakespeare, 1992, Sonnet 31)

The history of transference and integration are strongly present in this poem.

Humans, different from most other mammals, are born "too early", are totally helpless, and cannot survive without adequate maternal care. Bergmann (1988) writes,

> we need to love and be loved, because our prolonged childhood has revealed us as dependent on parental love. The original mother–child dyad was of such overwhelming significance that we yearn to refind it. . . . That the original dyad is subject to shock, stress, and trauma, is demonstrated in almost every analysis. There is, therefore, not only the yearning, but also a fear of the return of the infantile dependence. (p. 669)

Freud's *Three Essays* (1905d) already contained a theory of the diphasic nature of human sexuality. One aspect of this condition is that during latency, the sexual drive is split into two currents: the sensuous and the tender. The sensuous undergoes repression, while the tender remains conscious. During puberty, if all goes well, a new object replaces the old and the two currents are reunited. "Should these two currents fail to converge . . . the focusing of all desire upon a single object, will be unattainable" (Freud, 1905d, p. 200).

Freud (1921c, p. 90) stated,

> Libido is an expression taken from the theory of the emotions. We call by that name the energy, regarded as a quantitative magnitude . . . of those instincts which have to do with all that may be comprised under the word "love".

He had also (1914c) framed his concepts of primary narcissism and auto-eroticism in terms of the libido theory. Therefore, they all refer in this context only to vicissitudes (*Schicksalen*) of libidinally motivated forms of object seeking. However, Freud also considered that there are other, non-libidinal strivings in the baby. One cannot say either, that he saw the baby as merely narcissistic, objectless, and autoerotic in the original developmental state of affairs. On the contrary, he saw the ego instincts (*Ichtriebe*), which are identified with the self-preservative instincts and opposed to the sexual ones, as object related from the very beginning of the infantile life: "The first auto-erotic sexual satisfactions are experienced in connection with the vital functions which serve the purpose of self-preservation. The sexual instincts are at the outset attached to the satisfaction of the ego-instinct" (Freud, 1914c, p. 87). In 1915, he wrote that the self-preservative instincts "are never capable of auto-erotic satisfaction" (p. 134). I would add that this does not mean that a disordered or anxious person will not try to use auto-erotism for illusory "self-preservative" purposes.

Freud (1914c) struggled with the following question: is it necessary to distinguish a sexual libido from a non-sexual energy of the (self-preservative) ego instincts? In adulthood, sexual satisfaction is ideally achieved through the loving relationship with another, real person. A French proverb states this beautifully: in true love, spirit embraces body. But it is also possible that a serious cleavage has occurred during childhood between the self-preservative and libidinal drives, resulting in their chronic defusion. Freud, indeed, found the split between the affectionate and sensual currents, characteristic of the unresolved Oedipus complex:

> Two currents whose union is necessary to insure a completely normal attitude in love have, in the cases we are considering, failed to combine. These two may be distinguished as the affectionate and the sensual current. The affectionate current is the older of two. It springs from the earliest years of life; it is formed on the basis of the interests of the self-preservative instinct. (Freud, 1912d, pp. 180–183)

It is also an important question clinically as how they are integrated in the patient's love relations.

The split between love and desire in males Freud attributed to "an incestuous fixation on mother or sister which has never been surmounted" (Freud, 1912d, p. 180). Therefore, there are two images of mother: the Madonna and the whore. Paradoxically, men suffering from "psychical impotence seek objects which do not lead to love in order to keep their sensuality away from objects they love. The result is that where they love they do not desire and where they desire they cannot love" (p. 183). Freud also believed that the split between love and desire without actual impotence was far more widespread than commonly believed. He said also that love with an inhibited aim was, in fact, originally fully sensual love, and it is also in man's unconscious (p. 103).

Freud (1915b) wrote that love cannot be some kind of special component of the instinct of sexuality. He suggested that it should be reserved for the relation of the total ego to its object and as "the expression of the whole sexual current of feelings". This means that love can be applied only "after there has been a synthesis of all the components of instincts under the primacy of the genitals and in the service of reproduction" (pp. 133–138).

Diamond (2003; Diamond et al., 2007) argues that the sexual system is functionally independent of the attachment system. The systems themselves have different origins, functions, and underpinnings, although enduring love relations are used to integrate both affectionate and sensual currents.

Freud knew that he was extending the popular conception of sexuality in a way that was difficult to understand for everyman, because Freudian "sexuality" includes all sensual strivings and satisfactions. After the discovery of the dualistic drive theory, sexuality became metamorphosed into Plato's Eros, which includes object love as well as healthy narcissism. "In its essence", Freud (1921c) states, the 'Eros' of the philosopher Plato coincides exactly with the love-force, the libido, of psychoanalysis" (p. 91). In this way, Eros became a life force and seeking libido became, as a witness of its power, the indication of Eros.

Helen Fisher (2004) suggests that romantic love is one of three independent and interacting elements: sex drive, attachment, and attraction (or sexual preference, mate choice). Thus, the attraction, or mate choice, represents a third neural instinctual–emotional system (in addition to sexuality and attachment), which mediates some of the unique aspects of romantic love: the focused attention on specific gestures, the possessive "mate guarding", and the heightened motivation to win a preferred mating partner. However, we cannot conflate a neurobiological level of explanation of brain mechanisms with experiences of the subject constructing meanings on a psychological (behavioural) level because, as Marianne Leuzinger-Bohleber (2008, p. 153) rightly states, it would be a categorical mistake. They are two different "language games" (Wittgenstein).

Love and falling in love can also be experienced as a disturbance for mental balance. Then love only disturbs your peace and you ambivalently try to get rid of it. (The same is true of hate, for instance, in childhood towards your "bad" mother.) Karl Abraham was the first who explained that problem in his theory of depression (see May, 2001). Freud's dualistic drive theory was meant to explain how it is also possible to experience love as anxiety arousing and threatening. Thanatos seeks to eliminate its high tension or to reduce it to the lowest level possible (Nirvana principle), or, at least, to keep it unchanged (constancy principle). In Freud's original theory on binding instinctual energy (through a countercathexis) with its different forms is one derivative of Thanatos. Thanatos has a paradoxical double function: to destroy or to bind. Ikonen and Rechardt (2010) put it in this way: "Even as it destroys, it also strengthens psychic structures" (p. 100). According to Friedman (1992), Freud gave no concrete or value-bound content either to Eros or to Thanatos. They belong to the nature of human life, where "Todestrieb is mute and Eros is blind" (p. 320).

Is love a drive or an affect? If defined as a drive, it means that it must be primary and it has to be placed on the upper level of hierarchy, just like gravity in physics. Jonathan Lear (2003) argues in favour of love as a drive in his book, *Therapeutic Action*, by saying, "One reason that Freud's theory of love has been ignored is that it seems ridiculous to take seriously the idea that love is really a basic principle of nature" (p. 172). Socrates (in Plato's *Symposium*) tells that he heard the truth of love from a woman, Diotima. Love has a double nature and pulls men in two directions. Man loves what he does not own, what he is not, and what he is seeking. Love is desire, but desire means also that you are missing and seeking something in order to be able to feel yourself whole.

Primary love

The earliest development of narcissism takes place within the framework of maternal care. Alice Balint (1939) wanted to use the word primary love instead of primary narcissism. She found that mutual care is important for both the mother and her baby. The mother and the baby joyfully imitate each other. According to Ikonen (2000), too, the dynamic core in primary love is *a striving for mutuality*: that is, if the baby is happy, it gives pleasure to the mother, but if the baby is unhappy, it makes the mother unhappy also. To be successful, the mother has to have a capacity to empathise and complementarily recognise what is going on in her baby's mind and body. The psychic work with this striving for mutuality will later, more or less, be given up and replaced by a different kind of positive reciprocity (p. 31).

From the beginning of one's life, mirroring is extremely important, and it remains so in all love relationships. An old Finnish poem by Alli Nissinen (1909) nicely conveys its significance for the welfare of the child:

> Two are most beautiful in life, two true and lovely. Even if filled with grief, worry disappears, goes away. They are the stars of the night in my existence, they give me happiness. —Dear, lovable mother, look at me! Your eyes give me a blissful mind. (p. 27, translated for this edition)

Freud (1930a) described this kind of happy union in *Civilization and its Discontents*: "When a love-relationship is at its height there is no room left for any interest in the environment; a pair of lovers are sufficient to themselves, and do not even need the child they have in common to make them happy" (p. 108).

Narcissistic love relations

The lack of mutuality and reciprocity is strongly present in the Greek myth of Echo and Narcissus. As is known, both died. The first to die was Echo, unrecognised by Narcissus. In Freud's discovery of narcissism (1914c), love was seen as a progression from narcissistic libido to object libido. This transformation, as well as the projection of the ego ideal, Freud suggested, explains the overestimation of the love object by the lover. In this context, Freud postulated that human sexuality is essentially traumatic. Certain psychological problems are unavoidable.

Joyce McDougall (1985) describes how narcissistic problems might follow two distinct and, in appearance, widely different forms of expression as inevitable reactions to the trauma of otherness and to the obligation to assume a separate identity. Both forms follow the primitive mode of love and

> have their roots in the narcissistic sexuality of infancy, and each tries in hidden ways to maintain or recreate the primitive tie to the mother. For the self-object seekers, this object is sought in the external world. For those who defend themselves against the danger of the wish for a fusional self-objects, on the other hand, live this fusion in fantasy only. (pp. 223–224)

The fading of a narcissistic bond within the couple can also be a reason for a break-up. The depletion of narcissistic libido is common in pathological love. Grunberger (1979, p. 223) seems to think that "happiness is the expression of the subject's exclusive and megalomanical sense of enhancement by the object that has chosen him or her". It means that no object is sexually satisfying unless it also contributes to narcissistic enhancement.

According to Otto Kernberg (1995, p. 144)

> the oedipal resonance of all love relations causes the narcissistic person unconsciously to attempt a relationship dominated by aggression as much as or more than by love because of deep frustration and resentment from the past . . . [and] unconscious fear of the love object, related to projected aggression.

Such persons also show a remarkable absence of internal freedom to become interested in the true personality of the other. Dependency upon the other is feared and is replaced by self-righteous demandingness and frustration when demands are not met. In treatment, dependency on the therapist is experienced as humiliating and is defended against with attempts to omnipotently control the treatment (Kernberg, 2007, p. 506).

As a result of their ego weakness, "narcissists" cannot love anyone, neither themselves nor others. They give up the game because they do not have the courage to take the risk of putting their heart into it. Often, the entire aim of their activities is to strengthen their own grandiose self-image.

Oedipal love

Freud discovered the Oedipus complex in his self-analysis. In 1897, he wrote to Wilhelm Fliess as follows: "Only one idea of general value has occurred to me. I have found love of the mother and jealousy of the father in my own case too, and now believe it to be a general phenomenon of early childhood" (Freud, 1950, p. 223, letter 71).

According to Paul Ricoeur (1970, pp. 188–189), its universality is seen in the details of this singular experience:

> The Oedipus complex is the theory of seduction in reverse: the father does not seduce the child, but rather the child, in wishing to posses its mother, desires the death of the father. The seduction scene was transformed into a screen memory of the Oedipus complex, and the conflict of ambivalence became a source of a new kind of anxiety: castration anxiety.

That was the beginning of psychoanalysis (Freud, 1895d).

Ikonen (2000, p. 29) states that "oedipal love is really a great, often the greatest, emotion in man's life; our knowledge of true love is based upon this experience" (translated for this edition). But one can ask how this is possible, when we consider that the original oedipal phase results in tragedy with a narcissistic wound. Chasseguet-Smirgel (2005) wrote that the prematurity of the human infant prevents him from being incestuous from the outset, because of his prolonged genital incapacity. This prematurity is also at the origin of the Oedipus complex, which is connected not only with the sexual drive, but also with the need to be loved (p. 147). The Oedipus complex is a tragedy of smallness and inadequacy.

Real incest has nothing to do with oedipal love. In *Oedipus Rex* (Sophocles) Oedipus killed his father and married his mother. He was the son and husband of Jocasta and both the father and the brother of his children. Chasseguet-Smirgel (2005) stated that this is a staggering genealogy that clouds thought for a moment. She gave an illustration of this vertigo and its attack on the capacity to think: "a small 7-year-old girl was sexually abused by her godfather. The following day, she had forgotten how to count, as the teacher at her school observed" (p. 145). She continues by saying that "the castration anxiety that accompanies the Oedipus complex is a powerful factor in the transformation of the drives and, provided that it is not excessive, enables thought to unfold" (p. 147).

Chasseguet-Smirgel sees misogyny in modern psychoanalysis and says about the contemporary, relational school,

> the loving and caring of the relational theorists can only be a reference to the softness of the mother's breast, the path that leads there having been cleared of conflict, the sexual drive and possibly of thought itself. The modern utopias that liberate us from the body are never entirely able to escape the Oedipus complex, in its most archaic form, which is a quest for fusion with the mother through an elimination of all the obstacles in its path.

She concludes that "it is, therefore, no surprise to find that in these utopias, Freud, as someone who—like Oedipus—discovered some universal enigmas, should be the target of every attack" (p. 148).

Love and hate

Love as an affect is more often contrasted with hate than with fear. Who cannot hate, cannot love. Freud (1914c) stated that "the change of the content of an instinct into its opposite is observed in a single instance only – transformation of love into hate" (p. 133). For instance, in paranoia, love is transformed into hate, "I hate you", and finally into "You hate me".

Perhaps one of the greatest achievements in our field, or in Freud's legacy, is the realisation of how central the problem and tolerance of *ambivalence* is. With Freud, we find support in Goethe: when Faust says, "What is your name?" Mephisto answers, "The question seems absurd for someone who despises the mere word, who treats appearances as vain illusion and seeks the truth in such remote seclusion". And when Faust asks, "Who are you, then?", Mephisto answers, "A part of that same power that would forever work for evil, yet forever creates good" (Goethe, 1999, p. 42). The wisdom of this sentence tells us that without evil there will be no good, and without sin there would be no virtue.

How to avoid the distress of ambivalence? The process that compensates for the damage done to good objects by ambivalence is known as *reparation*. According to Melanie Klein, the depressive position has to do with the growth of whole objects through the mastery of ambivalence. Michael Balint (1952) emphasised the value of tenderness in integration. Mature love demands the capacity for concern, care, and mourning.

It is often just in exceptional and extreme phenomena that we discern the basic elements and regularities of normal life, for instance, in the various forms of psychopathology (Roos, 1986). In Medea's lines (1078–1081): "And I know what evil I am about to do, but my fury against Jason is stronger than my counsels of softness, and it is fury that leads to the greatest evils for mankind" (Euripides, 1998). Love does not manage to tame hate.

Happiness and love of truth

Should psychoanalysis always give us more happiness? According to Steven Mitchell (1998), the psychoanalytic interpretations have no value unless they promote the patient's personal happiness, sense of meaning, and dignity. Freud (1895d, pp. 253–306) thought that much is gained if we succeed in transforming hysterical misery into common unhappiness, but is the realistic appraisal of the love object a better guarantee of happiness than wish-fulfilling illusions?

In Freud's assessment in 1937, "the psychical apparatus is intolerant of unpleasure; it has to fend it off at all costs, and if the perception of reality entails unpleasure, that perception – the truth – must be sacrificed" (1937c, p. 237). For Bion (1965), that truth is essential for mental growth, since without it—when we lie—the psyche does not develop.

Love is the basic condition for any kind of virtue. Psychoanalysis can avoid falsehood only through its love of truth. It is this very attitude that makes possible the end of all delusion and betrayal. Freud's (1923a) original technical advice to the patient illustrates well the spirit of psychoanalysis in this regard: "truth and once again truth" (Freud, 1914c, in a letter to Putnam of 13 March). His words to Wortis (1954, p. 153) illustrate this commitment to truth: "I told you unpleasant things about yourself to show how honest one is in analysis". Honesty is more valuable than wishful thinking or belief.

The love of truth is also the most superior virtue in philosophy. Socrates thought that it must be above any other kind of love. Can we justify the value of truth in terms of its contribution to happiness? Socrates believed that through an examination of one's own soul, the truth would emerge and it would set one free. In his novel *Notes from Underground*, Fyodor Dostoyevsky (1972) wrote as follows:

> In every man's remembrances there are things he will not reveal to everybody, but only to his friends. There are other things he will not reveal even to his friends, but only himself, and then only under a pledge of secrecy. Finally, there are some things that a man is afraid to reveal even to himself, and any honest man accumulates a pretty fair number of such things. That is to say, the more respectable a man is, the more of them he has. (p. 45)

Love in psychoanalysis may have the same characteristics as in the love relationship of a couple, that is, identification and idealisation. A temptation to idealise and to become narcissistically attached to a certain theory can hinder seeing other possible perspectives (Roos, 1982, 2001). Our relationship to psychoanalysis might become an unhappy love relation if our unconscious aim is to get back our lost primary love: psychoanalysis in such cases risks becoming the equivalent of a religious faith, or ideology, and the narcissistic component in one's relation to theory might ultimately destroy the essential love of truth.

Freud said this in his paper on Wilhelm Jensen's *Gradiva*, when he saw a grain of truth concealed in Norbert Hanold's delusion that "we all attach our conviction to thought-contents in which truth is combined with error, and let it extend from the former over the latter" (Freud, 1907a, pp. 80–81). A Finnish artist, Juhana Blomstedt, will have the last word in this debate. He (siding with the demand for truthfulness that remains the psychoanalytic ideal) recently stated that if art no longer searches for truth, it does not deserve its name.

Love as cure

What is the difference between transference love and love outside the psychoanalysis? Freud (1915a) finds that the former

> is characterized by certain features which ensure it a special position In the first place it is provoked by the analytic situation; secondly, it is greatly intensified by the resistance, which dominates the situation; and thirdly, it is lacking to a high degree in a regard for reality. (p.168)

He states that the healing power of love against a delusion is not to be despised. Freud (1907a) compares "the method used by Gradiva to cure the delusion of her childhood friend to psychoanalytic investigation, which is an attempt to free up repressed love. The power of the past carries within it a principle of cure" (p. 22).

Ms A had a history of three previous failures in her love relations, until she, after some years in psychoanalysis, met the man of her dreams. He did not criticise or betray her as the previous men did. However, this new good relationship confused her and she began feel depressed and afraid of rejection by her new man. She slowly became conscious that she had never experienced this kind of happiness. Her relationship with her mother had not included proper emotional mutuality. This good man gave her what was missing in her childhood.

Transference love is the attempt to relive a much longed for infantile situation because it was once so happy, or is so sorely missed. Lear (1990) states that psychoanalysis leads to a better life through a particular deployment of the capacity for love.

Unhappy love

> Loveless marriages are horrible. But there is one thing worse than an absolutely loveless marriage: a marriage in which there is love, but on one side only; faith, but on one side only; devotion, but on one side only and in which of the two hearts one is sure to be broken. (Wilde, 1948, *An Ideal Husband*, p. 549)

Erikson (1968) noted that the secret of love is mutuality (p. 219). I think, therefore, that a serious obstacle to love is the denial (on the part of another) of mutual affirmation and disavowal of dependency needs. Without mirroring, love tends to die off.

Freud (1917e) wrote that "in the two most opposed situations of being most intensely in love and of suicide the ego is overwhelmed by the object, though in totally different ways" (p. 252). According to Bak (1973), when in love, the self is overwhelmed by the good object, and in suicide the self is overwhelmed by the bad object. In both cases, the object is taken into the self. Bak saw love as a midway state of mind, halfway between mourning and melancholia: the urgency of love comes from the need to avoid experiencing object loss. If the attempt to find a substitute for the lost person fails, love may turn into melancholia or suicide. Goethe's Werther, Flaubert's Madame Bovary, and Tolstoy's Anna Karenina are the outstanding examples of such love suicides in world literature.

There are countless ways a happy love can be turned into a hell, the latter of which means suffering because you are not able to love any more. As Benvulio exclaims in *Romeo and Juliet*, Act I, scene I):

> Alas, that love, so gentle in his view,
> Should be so tyrannous and rough in proof!
>
> (Shakespeare, 1992)

Experiencing the self as unworthy of love is common in many kinds of psychopathology, especially in borderline states, narcissistic personality disorders, depression, and masochistic conditions. Often the lovers (mostly unconsciously) wish that their partners will heal all the wounds from previous love relations. Klein (1937, p. 322) observed that with people who are so over-dependent on others, love is very much needed as a support against the sense of guilt and fears of various kinds. Hence, the loved person, through demonstrating affection, must endlessly prove that they are not rejecting, not aggressive, and that (the subject's) destructive impulses have not taken effect.

When unhappily in love, blind repetition of the past is often conspicuous. Dicks (1967) found that the couples he studied established a compromise formation between their re-enacted unconscious, pathogenic object relations and their conscious wishes, mutual expectations, and idealisations. Unhappiness resulted because a desired and needed object relationship in the inner world, which the partner was cast to implement, was not fulfilled. Dicks observed that his subjects would persecute the very tendencies in their spouses that originally attracted them, since the partner was unconsciously perceived as a symbol of the "lost", ambivalently loved object. In jealousy paranoia, the more rigid or unwilling to express tender emotions the spouse is, the more disturbed is the jealous individual (Roos, 1971).

There are several reasons for an inability to love: failures of attachment in the symbiotic phase, traumatic separations, too many carers, an inability to mutually share, and illnesses. All of these experiences may hinder later refinding, processes may become severely hindered, and the road back to the primary object and to mutuality and gratifying intimacy is blocked. To add another metapsychological elucidation of this, we can go to Edith Jacobson (1964), who stressed that if the ego ideal as a separate structure has not developed and tension between ego and ego ideal is lacking, wishful images of the self predominate, as may be observed in narcissistic personalities driven repeatedly to fall in love.

The affect of love can be both strong and fragile. It is somehow similar to man's health, which also can deteriorate quickly and dramatically. To heal one's wounded love is not a simple matter. It seems that the unfortunate individual who has lost his love can, in real life, be healed only by a new love after an appropriate work of sorrow.

Concluding remarks: happy love

Both Freud (1905d) and Klein (1957) understood love as being derived from the infant's relationship to the breast. For Klein, the infant's feeling of bliss at being suckled is the basis for the future capacity for love, gratitude, and all happiness. She also thought that the baby is capable of love.

According to Aristotle (1963),

> happiness is good activity, not amusement. . . . evidently happiness must be placed among those desirable in themselves, not among those desirable for the sake of something else; for happiness does not lack anything, but is self-sufficient. (p. 261)

Those who love maturely, accepting the separateness of the others, have an integrated sense of self, object constancy, and a solidly established, healthy flow of secondary narcissism. However, all love relations involve the attribution of qualities to the other that are created by the subject. Transference is one obvious example of this. Singer (1966) calls this aspect of love the object *bestowal* (whereas the appraisal of the object is acknowledgment of its real, distinct attributes). In transitional object relations, the object as a whole is created by the subject. To Robert Waelder (1930), love represented an act of integration of a very high order, a combination of "physical gratification with a happy relationship" (2007, p. 80). He described love as a tribute to the ego's capacity to bring together harmoniously the wishes of the id, the demands of the repetition compulsion and of the superego, and the claims of reality. The ideal love object found or chosen is sexually gratifying, connected unconsciously to love objects in the person's past, sufficiently admired to meet the approval of the ego ideal, and appropriate in meeting the demands of reality.

Love is, in fact, a simultaneous attempt to refind something old and to find someone new. When it leads to a happy result, it is able to integrate coherently the bliss from the much longed for state of primary love (before separation and individuation), mirroring of the self in the beloved, refinding of the early (pre-oedipal and oedipal) love object simultaneously in later developmental phases, improving on the old love by finding someone new (greatly missed, but experienced as someone never met before, especially during childhood), repairing the internal damaged object by confronting and working through guilt feelings. It is said that to be content with little is true happiness; that a happy man is rich enough.

In love, through identification and idealisation, the well-being of the other becomes as important as one's own. In a happy love relationship, it is possible to consciously or unconsciously integrate deep erotic passion, mutual intimacy, honesty and trust, feelings of care, hope, and safety, reciprocal understanding, and sharing of experience. The integrative power of love invites wonder and reflection. The more love there is, the more wisdom there will be.

References

Aristotle (1963). *The Nicomachean Ethics*, D. Ross (Trans.). London: Oxford University Press.

Bak, R. C. (1973). Being in love and object choice. *International Journal of Psychoanalysis, 54*: 1–8.

Balint, A. (1939). Love for the mother and mother love. In: M. Balint, *Primary Love and Psycho-Analytic Technique* (pp. 109–127). London: Maresfield Library, 1952.

Balint, M. (1952). *Primary Love and Psycho-Analytic Technique*. London: Maresfield Library.

Bergmann, M. S. (1980). On the intrapsychic function of falling in love. *Psychoanalytic Quarterly, 49*: 56–76.

Bergmann, M. S. (1982). Platonic love, transference love, and love in real life. *Journal of the American Psychoanalytic Association, 30*: 87–111.

Bergmann, M. S. (1988). Freud's three theories of love in the light of later developments. *Journal of the American Psychonalytic Association, 36*: 653–672.

Bion, W. R. (1965). *Transformations*. London: Heinemann.

Bruckner, P. (2012). *The Paradox of Love*, S. Rendall (Trans.). Oxford: Princeton University Press.

Chasseguet-Smirgel, J. (2005). *The Body as Mirror of the World*. London: Free Association Books.

Diamond, D., Blatt, S. J., & Lichtenberg, J. D. (2007). *Attachment & Sexuality*. London: Analytic Press.

Diamond, L. M. (2003). What does sexual orientation orient? A biobehavioral model distinguishing romantic love and sexual desire. *Psychology Review, 110*: 173–229.

Dicks, H. (1967). *Marital Tensions*. New York: Basic Books.

Dostoyevsky, F. (1972). *Notes from Underground* (1946). London: Penguin.

Erikson, E. H. (1968). *Identity. Youth and Crisis*. New York: Norton.

Euripides (1998). *Medea and Other Plays*, J. Morwood (Trans.). Oxford: Oxford University Press.

Fisher, H. (2004). *Why We Love: The Nature and Chemistry of Romantic Love*. New York: Holt.

Fonagy, P. (2008). A genuinely developmental theory of sexual enjoyment and its implications for psychoanalytic technique. *Journal of the American Psychoanalytic Association, 56*(1): 11–36.

Freud, S. (1895d). *Studies on Hysteria. S. E., 2*. London: Hogarth.

Freud, S. (1905d). *Three Essays on the Theory of Sexuality. S. E., 7*: 125–245. London: Hogarth.

Freud, S. (1907a). Delusions and dreams in Jensen's "Gradiva". *S. E., 9*: 3–95 London: Hogarth.

Freud, S. (1912d). On the universal tendency to debasement in the sphere of love. *S. E., 11*: 179–190. London: Hogarth.

Freud, S. (1914c). On narcissism: an introduction. *S. E., 14*: 67–101. London: Hogarth.

Freud, S. (1915a/1914). Observations on transference-love. *S. E.*, *12*: 157–171. London: Hogarth.

Freud, S. (1915b). Instincts and their vicissitudes. *S. E.*, *14*: 111–140. London: Hogarth.

Freud, S. (1917e/1915). Mourning and melancholia. *S. E.*, *14*: 239–258. London: Hogarth.

Freud, S. (1920g). *Beyond the Pleasure Principle. S .E.*, *18*: 7–64. London: Hogarth.

Freud, S. (1921c). *Group Psychology and the Analysis of the Ego. S. E.*, *18*: 67–143. London: Hogarth.

Freud, S. (1923a). Two encyclopedia articles. *S. E.*, *18*: 233–260. London: Hogarth.

Freud, S. (1926d). *Inhibitions, Symptoms and Anxiety. S. E.*, *20*: 77–174. London: Hogarth.

Freud, S. (1930a). *Civilization and its Discontents. S. E.*, *21*: 59–145. London: Hogarth.

Freud, S. (1937c). Analysis terminable and interminable. *S. E.*, *23*: 211–253. London: Hogarth.

Freud, S. (1950). *The Origins of Psycho-Analysis*. London: Imago.

Friedman, L. (1992). Freud's Todestrieb: Part II. *International Journal of Psychoanalysis*, *19*: 309–322.

Goethe, J. W. von (1999). *Faust. A Tragedy in Two Parts*. London: Bibliophile Books.

Green, A. (1995). Has sexuality anything to do with psychoanalysis? *International Journal of Psychoanalysis*, *76*: 871–878.

Grunberger, B. (1979). *Narcissism: Psychoanalytic Essays*. New York: International Universities Press.

Hitschmann, E. (1952). Freud's conception of love. *International Journal of Psychoanalysis*, *33*: 421–428.

Ikonen, P. (2000). *Psykoanalyyttisia tutkielmia* (Psychoanalytic Studies). Helsinki: Yliopistopaino.

Ikonen, P. (2004). A brief inquiry into the value of man. In: A. Laine (Ed.), *Power of Understanding. Essays in Honour of Veikko Tähkä* (pp. 217–223). London: Karnac.

Ikonen, P., & Rechardt, E. (2010). *Thanatos, Shame, and Other Essays*. London: Karnac.

Jacobson, E. (1964). *The Self and the Object World*. New York: International Universities Press.

Kernberg, O. F. (1995). *Love Relations. Normality and Pathology*. London: Yale University Press.

Kernberg, O. F. (2007). The almost untreatable narcissistic patient. *Journal of the American Psychoanalytic Association, 55*(2): 503–539.

Klein, M. (1937). Love, guilt and reparation. In: *Love, Guilt and Reparation and Other Works* (Volume 1) (pp. 306–343). New York: Free Press, 1975.

Klein, M. (1957). *Envy and Gratitude.* London: Tavistock.

Lear, J. (1990). *Love and its Place in Nature. A Philosophical Interpretation of Freudian Psychoanalysis.* New York: Faber.

Lear, J. (2003). *Therapeutic Action. An Earnest Plea for Irony.* London: Karnac.

Leuzinger-Bohleber, M. (2008). Commentary on "Is there a drive to love?" *Neuro-Psychoanalysis, 10*: 149–154.

May, U. (2001). Abraham's discovery of the 'bad mother'. A contribution to the history of the theory of depression. *International Journal of Psychoanalysis, 82*: 283–305.

McDougall, J. (1985). *Theatres of the Mind: Illusion and Truth on the Psychoanalytic Stage.* New York: Basic Books.

Mitchell, S. A. (1988). *Relational Concepts in Psychoanalysis. An Integration.* Boston, MA: Harvard University Press.

Nissinen, A. (1909). Hopeakauha. In: E. Salola & E. Keskinen (Eds.), *Lausunta- runoja nuorelle väelle* (p. 27). Helsinki: Valistus, 1951.

Plato (1964). Symposium. *The Collected Dialogues of Plato.* New York: Pantheon.

Ricoeur, P. (1970.) *Freud and Philosophy. An Essay on Interpretation*, D. Savage (Trans.). London: Yale University Press.

Roos, E. (1971). Pathological communication and object-relations of marital jealousy. *Psychiatria Fennica*, 139–160.

Roos, E. (1982). Psychoanalysis and the growth of knowledge. *Scandinavian Psychoanalytic Review*, 5: 183–199.

Roos, E. (1986). The part analysis plays in psychoanalysis. A historical perspective. *Scandinavian Psychoanalytic Review*, 9: 31–55.

Roos, E. (2001). Changing scientific idols and ideals in the history of psychoanalysis. *Psychoanalysis in Europe, Bulletin*, 55: 147–155.

Shakespeare, W. (1992). *The Illustrated Stratford Shakespeare.* London: Chancellor Press.

Singer, L. (1966). *The Nature of Love: Plato to Luther.* New York: Random House.

Stendhal (1822). *On Love.* New York: Penquin Classics, 1975.

Waelder, R. (1930). The principle of multiple function: observations on overdetermination. Reprinted in 2007 in *Psychoanalytic Quarterly*, 1: 75–92.

Widlöcher, D. (2002). Primary love and infantile sexuality: an eternal debate. In: D. Widlöcher (Ed.), *Infantile Sexuality and Attachment* (pp. 1–35). New York: Other Press.

Wilde, O. (1948). *Complete Works of Oscar Wilde*. London: Collins.

Wortis, J. (1954). *Fragments of an Analysis with Freud*. New York: Jason Aronson.

INDEX

abortion, xiv, 9, 13–14, 69, 79
Abraham, K., 157
affect(ive), 4, 44, 59, 89, 134–135, 140,
    144, 157, 161
  aggression/aggressive, 88
  deeply, xiii
  expressions of, 131
  negative, 3
  of love, 166
  painful, 44, 145
  reactions, 131, 145
  regulation, 4
  traumatic, 145
aggression/aggressive, 36, 54–59,
    61–62, 81–82, 88, 91–92, 94–95,
    112, 124, 147, 159, 165
    see also: affect(ive), woman
  drive impulse, 3
  energy, 56, 88, 94, 99
  excessive, 56
  female, 68
  impulse, 59
  inhibited, 95

insufficient, 56
intractable, 145
negative, 59
projected, 159
unconscious(ness), 147–148
violent, xiv
wish, 145
Alizade, M., 54, 58
Amaniti, M., 4
ambivalence, 10–11, 16, 53–54,
    59, 61–64, 149, 157, 160, 162,
    166
  complex, 10
  distress of, 162
  early, 53
  feelings, 53, 59
  love, 60
    –hate, 57
  maternal, xiv, 54, 81
  pre-, 15
  tolerance of, 82, 161
  woman's, 70
André, J., 125

anger, 3, 14, 22, 31, 54–55, 66, 70, 72,
    76, 78, 82, 92, 100, 118, 144,
    149
    unconscious(ness), 144
anxiety, 1, 8, 33, 59, 125, 136, 140, 142,
    145, 155, 157
    annihilation, 147
    archaic, 6
    castration, 122–123, 125, 127,
        160–161
    powerful, 123
    separation, 104, 123, 142
    severe, 10
Aphrodite, 38
Aristotle, xiii, 44, 152, 166
Arlow, J., xiii
attachment, 3, 60, 68, 130, 157, 166
    affectionate, 153
    deep, 110
    system, 156
    trauma, 86
attraction, 157
Auerhahn, N. C., 15
autoerotism, 155
autonomy, 63, 78, 99

Bachman, J., 86
badness, xv, 86–89, 91–92
Bak, R. C., 165
Balint, A., 158
Balint, M., 61, 162
behaviour, 60, 86, 89, 95, 116, 135, 157
    violent, 85–86
Bergmann, M. S., 152–154
Bible, The, 60
Bion, W. R., 58, 148, 162
Blatt, S. J., 156
Blomstedt, J., 163
body image
    fragile, 123
    unlovable, 125
    shameful, 126
Böhm, T., 144
Buonaparte, M., 29
Bovary, E., 165

Bowlby, J., 130
breastfeeding, 5, 8, 55, 61–62, 65, 79,
    105
Brown, L. M., 86
Bruckner, P., 151
Brunswick, R., 29
Burch, B., 104, 121
Burlingham, D., xv, 119–121, 130
Butler, J., 126

case vignettes
    Ada, 104–110, 116, 121–122,
        126–127
    Claire, 70
    Dora, 37–38
    Kirsti, 131–149
    Leena, 70–71
    Lucia, 30–31, 35
    Maija, 70
    Mrs B, 3, 5–8, 15, 17
    Mrs C, 18
    Ms A, 164
    Ms E, 10–15
    Rita, 34
    Sara, 33–35
    Silvia, 22–26, 28, 32
    Teresa, 69
catastrophe, 2, 7, 46–47, 50, 119, 140,
    145, 147
Chasseguet-Smirgel, J., 122–123,
    160–161
Chesney-Lind, M., 86
civilisation, 16, 25, 36, 60, 62,
    152–153
Claus, J., 48
closed system, 146
Colchis, 30–31, 37–39, 72
conscious(ness), xiii, 23, 41, 49, 68,
    86, 99, 110–111, 118, 140, 148,
    155, 164–165, 167 see also:
    unconscious(ness)
contain, 8, 63, 82, 92, 106, 108, 124,
    148
    lack of, 148
    un-, 59

countertransference, xv, 38, 143
    see also: transference
  feelings, 105–106
    negative, 3
    unbearable, 2–3
couple, xiv, 9–10, 15–18, 24, 27, 35, 79,
    130, 159, 163, 165
  childless, 79
  divided, 27
  fleeing, 2
  normal, 8
  sexual, 103
  young, 31
Covington, C., 57
creativity, xiii–xiv, 23, 25–26, 36,
    56–58, 113, 124
crisis intervention, 10, 13, 15–16
Cronenberg, D., 58

De Lauretis, T., 104, 121, 125–126
death, 2, 5, 7, 15, 17, 48, 55, 72, 89, 93,
    95–96, 107–109, 117–119, 141
    see also: depression, *Thanatos*,
    wish
  drive, 55–59, 63, 73, 86–89,
    94–95
  fear of, 140, 147
  imminent, 43
  instinct, xv, 152
  metaphors of, 107
  of child, 15, 40, 43
  of father, 5, 160
  of mother, 13–14
  of sister, 7, 117
  of unborn baby, 4, 8–9, 12, 15
  psychic(al), 147
defence, 127, 144–145
  central, 147
  effective, 146
  manic, 24
  methods, 53
  narcissistic, 6, 145
  rigid, 114
  self-, 57
  strategies, 15

  strong, 149
  unconscious(ness), 15
delusion, 163–164
dénouement, 48
dependency, 15, 32, 76, 120,
    159–160
depression, 10–11, 13, 22, 26, 33–35,
    56, 64, 66, 72, 76, 82, 95, 121, 142,
    164–165 *see also*: world
  death-like, 109
  deep, 144
  illness, 3
  inner, 142
  maternal, 3–4, 36, 109, 111–112,
    120–121
  position, 87, 89, 98–99, 162
  postpartum, 79, 106
  psychotic, 121
  severe, 3–5, 67
  theory of, 157
destructive(ness), xiii, 36, 53–56,
    58–59, 68, 71, 75, 77, 88
  action, 58
  aspects, 77
  drives, 62, 86, 88, 99
  fantasy, 3, 62
  female, 1–2, 15
  impulses, xv, 1–2, 165
  potential, 8
  revenge, 73
  tendencies, 147
  thoughts, 67
Deutsch, H., 29
development(al), xiv, 50, 57, 61, 79,
    87, 91, 93, 98–99, 146–148, 151,
    155
  acquisition, 89
  female, 38
  normal, 8
  oedipal, 94–96
  of basic trust, 77
  of narcissism, 158
  phases, 167
  process, 61
  result, 99

self-, 3
sexual, 123
social, 58
stage, 145
theory of, 153
Diamond, D., 156
Diamond, L. M., 156
Dicks, H., 165–166
Diotima, 158
disappointment, 53, 59, 66–67, 75–77,
    98, 111, 114, 118, 123–124,
    138–139, 144, 148–149, 151
Disney, W., 91–92
Dostoyevsky, F., 163
dreams, 6, 23, 29, 35, 69, 73, 164
drive *see also*: death, life
    antagonistic, 56
    constructive, 99
    creative, 151
    destructive, 62, 86, 88, 99
    ego, 88
    erotic, 58, 62
    impulses, 3
    libidinal, 155
    sexual, 88, 153–154, 157, 160–161
    theory, 153
        dualistic, 86, 88, 156–157

Echo, 159
ego, 57–59, 61, 88, 109, 122–123, 125,
    152, 154, 165–166 *see also*: drive
    bodily, 113
    capacity, 167
    faltering, xiv
    ideal, 75, 99, 106, 159, 166–167
    instinct, 155
    libido, 126
    self-observing, 145
    super-, 75, 89, 167
    synthesis, xiv
    total, 156
    weakness, 160
emotion(ally), xiii, 4, 6, 18, 27, 32, 34,
    44–45, 59, 110, 145, 155, 160
    bond, 27

cleansing, 44
conflicting, 54
disturbing, 27
experiences, 143–144
frozen, 3
intensity, 22, 31
maltreated, 86
maternal, 120
mutuality, 164
overwhelming, 18
system, 157
taxing, 15
tender, 166
theory of, 62
Empedocles, 86
emptiness, xv, 66, 106, 130, 143–144,
    146–147
Enckell, H., xiii
Engels, E.-M., 2, 9, 15, 17–18
envy, 26–27, 50, 60, 71, 77, 88–90,
    94–95, 98–99, 103
    attack, 23
    intensive, 77
    of breast, 87
    unbearable, 90
Erikson, E. H., 165
Eros, 2, 38–39, 50, 55, 58, 61–62,
    86, 88, 99, 109, 152,
    156–157
*Ethical Dilemma Due to Prenatal and
    Genetic Diagnostics* (EDIG), 9–10,
    12, 15, 17
Euripides, xiii–xiv, 17, 21–22,
    25, 27, 32, 35, 37–40, 43–51,
    72, 74–75, 95, 162
evacuation, 129–130, 145,
    147–148
externalisation, xiii

Faimberg, H., 15
fairy tales, 77–78, 89, 92, 94, 99
    Cinderella, xv, 96
    Little Snow-White, xv, 89–94, 99
    Mother Holle, xv, 96–99
    Sleeping Beauty, xv, 89, 92–94

fantasy, 7, 47, 87, 94, 98, 104, 107–110, 112, 125 *see also*: destructive(ness), infantile, Medea, unconscious(ness), world
  day-dream, 2
  detailed, 3
  female, 16
  primal scene, 117
  sexual, 7–8
  sister, xv, 104, 106, 108, 110, 118–122, 126–127
  system, 2
  twin, 119
father, 2, 5–6, 11–12, 17, 29, 31–32, 40, 55, 57, 62, 70, 73, 94–96, 99, 108–109, 111–112, 117, 120, 123–125, 131, 136–137, 140, 147, 160–161 *see also*: death, oedipal
  god-, 161
  grand, 39–40, 47
  horrified, 42
  idolised, 120
  possessive, 120
Faucher, E., 70
fears, 24, 68–69, 71, 73, 77, 85, 109, 112, 116, 165
female, xv, 3, 7–8, 24, 32, 109, 115, 117, 123, 125 *see also*: development(al), fantasy, transference
  analysands, 8
  characters, 43
  core identity, 8
  destructiveness, xiii, 1–2, 15
  figure, 1
  homosexuality, 124
  ideals, xiv
  identity, 15, 103
  masochism, xiv, 36
  mind, 30
  objects, 124
  patients, 1, 3–4
  problem, 26

  self, 8
  -representation, 1
  society, 57
  structure, 35
  truth, 4
femininity, xiv, 1–3, 8, 25–26, 29–30, 66, 94, 109, 113, 119–120, 127
  dark continent of, 3
fetish, xv, 104, 108–109, 122–123, 125–127
Fischer, G., 15
Fischmann, T., 9
Fisher, H., 157
Flaubert, G., 165
Fletcher, J. C., 17
Fonagy, P., 89, 153
Frankenstein, 67
fratricide, 48
Freud, A., xv, 104, 119–121, 127, 130
Freud, M., 119
Freud, S. (*passim*)
  cited works, 2, 15–16, 29, 37–38, 41, 45, 53, 56, 60–62, 86, 88, 93, 122, 124, 126, 152–156, 158–166
Friedman, L., 157
friendship, 70, 110, 116, 118, 120–121, 127
  close, xv
  intense, 110, 114
  mutual, 70
  passionate, 116
  platonic, 115
  same sex, xv, 70, 110, 114–116, 118, 120–121, 127
frustration, 50, 149, 159
fusion, 62–63, 159, 161
  chronic, 155
  illusion of, 67
  monetary, 59
  symbiotic, 67, 106, 110

Garland, C., 144
Gertzi, S., 145
Glaser, B., 130

Goethe, J. W. von, 161–162, 165
    Faust, 161–162
    Werther, 165
Golden Fleece, 2, 25, 36, 39, 72
Goodkind, S., 86
goodness, xv, 86, 88–91, 98
Gradiva, 163–164
Green, A., 58, 112–113, 121, 153
Greenacre, P., 123
grief, 73, 79–80, 111, 149, 158
Grimm, J., 89–92, 96
Grimm, W., 89–92, 96
grounded theory, 130, 143
Grunberger, B., 159
guilt, 12–14, 26, 47–48, 55, 57, 64–65,
    67, 69, 71, 74, 80, 87, 92, 96, 100,
    118, 147, 165, 167

happiness, 60, 67, 140, 151–153,
    158–159, 162–164, 166–167
    marital, 46
    search for, xv
hate, xiv, 44, 54, 57, 59, 61–62, 67, 77,
    82, 95, 98, 151, 157, 161–162
Heide, K. M., 86
helplessness, xv, 4, 76, 80, 89, 144,
    146, 149, 153
hermeneutics, xiv
hero, 2, 21, 25–26, 35–36, 41, 44,
    47–48, 96
heroine, xiii, 40, 42, 46, 89, 95
Hildt, E., 9
Hitschmann, E., 153
holding, 8, 23, 34, 56, 62, 121, 134,
    143
honour, 22, 42, 72, 75, 81, 96

idealisation, 27, 50, 130, 146, 163, 165,
    167
identification, 27, 89–91, 94, 98–99,
    103, 125–126, 163, 167
    crossed, 30
    masculine, 28
    object of, 8
    projective, 28, 131

identity, 1, 28, 32–34, 36, 39, 54, 87,
    89, 122, 125–126
    core, 8
    crisis, 40
    female, 15, 103–104
    loss of, 34, 40
    separate, 159
    stable, 8
    true, 49
ideology, 163
Ikonen, P., 58, 75, 86, 88, 152,
    157–158, 160
illusion, 24, 54, 67, 78, 105, 110, 117,
    119, 127, 162
    childhood, 75
    flattering, 152
    narcissistic, 126
    of perfection, 108, 112–113, 122
    bodily, 110, 125
    vain, 162
incest, 152, 156, 160–161
Inderbitzin, L. B., 2
infancy, 94, 159
infanticide, 48, 55
infantile
    day-dream, 2
    dependence, 154
    life, 155
    love, xv
    neurosis, 5
    paradise, 5
    sexual, 153
        fantasy, 8
    situation, 164
    trauma, 145
instinct, 62, 155–156, 161 see also:
        death, ego
    energy, 157
    maternal, 65
    neuronal, 157
    self-preservative, 155–156
    sexual, 155–156
integration, 3, 95, 113–114, 120, 154,
    162, 167
internalise, xiv, 144

Jacobson, E., 166
Janssen, H. J., 17
jealousy, 38, 89–90, 103, 116–117, 160, 166
Jensen, W., 163
Jesus, 47
Johnston, S. I., 48
Jonze, S., 106

Kaplan, S., 133, 137, 144–145
Kaven, P., 129
Kernberg, O. F., 159–160
Klein, M., 15, 30, 87, 90, 162, 165–166
Kohut, H., 104
Kristeva, J., 108, 121
Krystal, M. D., 135, 145

Lacan, J., 58, 108
Lampl-de Groot, J., 29
Langer, M., 17
language games, 157
Laplanche, J., 58
Lasker, J. N., 17
Laub, D., 15
Lear, J., 157, 164
Lehtonen, J., 4
lesbian(ism), 125–126
    desire, 125
    gaze, 126
    eroticism, 115
    libido, 124
    love, 104, 121, 124–126
    orientation, 107, 124
    phallus, 126
    relationship, 120
    women, 127
Leuzinger-Bohleber, M., 1–2, 4, 9–10, 15, 17–18, 68, 157
libido, 3, 8, 55, 59, 61–62, 112–113, 117, 124, 152, 155, 157 see also: ego, lesbian(ism), sexual
    homosexual, 107, 124
    narcissistic, 159
    object(ive), 126, 159
    theory, 155

Lichtenberg, J. D., 156
lie, 49, 162
life (passim) see also: Eros
    companion, 25
    cycle, xiv, 86, 88
    drive, 55–56, 58, 73, 86–88, 94, 99
    erotic, 152
    eventful, 125
    force, 54, 70–71, 115, 151, 157
    human, xv, 86, 153, 157
    infantile, 155
    internal, 32
    isolated, 5
    joy of, 21, 23, 27
    -less, 5, 47
    new, 47
    normal, 18, 145, 162
    past, 43
    quality, 18
    real, 45
    restricted, 5
    secluded, 110
    sexual, 33, 107
    social, 64, 118
    threatening, 109
    transience of, 93
    withdrawn, 5
    working, 75, 81
Lindgren, A., 103
love (passim) see also: infantile, lesbian(ism), maternal, transference
    ambivalent, 60
    anaclictic, 60, 153
    as cure, 164
    -child, 111
    considerate, 59
    early, 60
    erotic, 64, 114
    excited, 61
    expectations of, 94
    for beauty, 62
    for mankind, 62
    genital, 60, 153
    happy, 151, 165–167

healthy, 60
heterosexual, 121
ideal, 59–60
impossible, 116
mature, 162, 166
narcissistic, 59–61, 118, 126, 153
object(ive), 2, 56, 60–61, 94, 108,
    112, 123, 126, 152–154, 156,
    159, 162, 166–167
oedipal, 160–161
parent(al), 154
partner, 2, 15
pathological, 159
physical, 115
positive, 55
possessive, 118
primary, 59, 61, 158, 163, 167
primitive, 59, 61
psychology of, xv, 60
relationship, 61, 124, 152–153, 156,
    158–159, 163–166
repressed, 164
romantic, 63, 157
sexual, 59, 61–62
sibling, 62
sisterly, 114, 117, 127
symbiotic, 56, 105–106, 108, 112,
    114
tender, 62
theory of, 158
true, 160
unhappy, 151–152, 163–165
wounded, 166

Madonna, 33, 54, 156
Maliniemi-Piispanen, S., 148
Maran, G., 89
masculine, 24, 48, 76, 126
    desire, 126
    fields of interest, 50
    identification, 28
    order, 49
    power, 42, 49, 117
    pursuits, 75
    world, 42, 50

masochism, xiv, 26, 29, 32, 36, 63, 95,
    165
    female, 36
    sado-, 146
masturbation, 107
maternal, 31, 76 see also: depression,
    instinct, object
    ambivalence, xiv
    care, 77, 154, 158
    desires, 64, 107
    function, 54
    ideals, 75
    love, 63
Mattsson, B., 148
May, U., 65, 157
McDougall, J., 123–124, 143,
    159
Medea (passim) see also: crisis
    intervention, phantasy
    characterisation, 17
    fantasy, xiv, 1–2, 4, 7–9,
    15–17
melancholy, 58, 118, 121, 165
    gloominess, 105
memory, 21, 25, 35–36, 131, 133–137,
    145, 148, 160
Menozzi, F., 4
mental, 125
    balance, 49, 157
    disturbances, 54, 151
    growth, 162
    phenomenon, 45
    picture, 135
    space, 131
    state, 10, 151
    violence, 54, 56, 59, 78
    vulnerability, 49
Mephisto, 162
metaphor, xiii, 107, 117
Miller, E., 130
mirror, 35, 104, 112–113, 119, 158,
    165, 167
    analytical, 34
    false, 113–114
    image, 104, 113, 118, 122, 126

magic, 90
    positive, 119
    reflecting, 118
misogyny, 161
Mitchell, S. A., 162
mother (*passim*) *see also*: oedipal
    bad, 78, 81, 91, 157
    –child relationship, 38, 65, 71, 91,
        123, 130, 154
    depressed, 4, 36, 109, 111–112,
        120–121
    good, 34, 75, 77, 94
        -enough, 8, 98
    ideal(ised), 33, 75–77, 94
    image of, 91
    murdering, xiv, 68
    narcissistic, 24
    rebel, 30
    trauma(tic), 3–4
mourning, 22, 24, 58, 71, 108, 111,
    121, 148, 162, 165
mutuality, 158–159, 164–169
myth, xiii–xv, 1–3, 6, 30, 36–37, 39,
    46–47, 68, 71, 80, 95–96, 98,
    159
    ancient, 37, 94
    figures, 48
    motherly, 76–77, 79

narcissistic, 7, 34–35, 104, 123, 155,
    159–160, 163, 166 *see also*:
    defence, development(al),
    libido, love, mother,
    vulnerability
    bad, 63
    bond, 159
    component, 118, 163
    desire, 26
    discovery of, 159
    enhancement, 159
    good, 63
    healthy, 156
    illusion, 126
    injury, 2
    omnipotence, 112

perfection, 106
    personality disorder, 165
    primary, 121, 155, 158
    problems, 159
    pursuits, 66
    rage, 2
    satisfaction, 8
    secondary, 166
    selfishness, 63
    sexuality, 159
    traits, 144
    wound, 76, 111–113, 126, 144,
        160
Narcissus, 159
Nietzsche, F., 40–41, 45, 112
Nippert, G., 17
Nirvana principle, 157
Nissinen, A., 158
Novick, J., 146
Novick, K. K., 146

object(ive), 18, 31, 33, 53, 58–59,
    62, 70, 88, 94, 103, 107–109,
    112, 117, 124, 126, 134, 142,
    148–149, 153–156, 159, 165,
    167 *see also*: libido, love,
    self
    bad, 87, 90, 165
    bestowal, 166
    boundaries, 6
    choice, 124–125
    constancy, 166
    damaged, 167
    external, 61
    fetish, 126
    good, 162, 165
    indestructible, 3
    inner, 144
    loss, 121, 165
    love, 2, 56, 60–61, 112, 123, 126,
        152–153, 156, 166–167
    maternal, 8
    of identification, 89, 91, 94
    primary, 3, 112, 144, 166
    real, 31

relations, 2–4, 8, 17, 58, 155, 165
  history, 17
  pathogenic, 165
  theory, 17, 153
  transitional, 167
representation, 87, 90
seeking, 155
transitional, 122
whole, 87, 162
Odysseus, 48
oedipal, 167 see also: development(al),
    love
  competition, 57
  dimension, 6
  disavowal, 126
  father, 98–99
  girl, 98
  loneliness, 62
  monsters, 31
  mother, 7, 91, 94, 98
  phase, 17, 94, 160
  position, 123
  pre-, 167
  resonance, 159
  script, 125
  setting, 103, 108, 112, 127
  triangle, 57, 122
Oedipus, 47, 68, 161
  complex, 57, 125–126, 155, 160–161
  myth, 71
Ogden, T. H., 87–88
Oliner, M., 15
Olshansky, D., 57
Olsson, H., 104, 110, 114–116, 118,
    120
O'Malley, P., 86
orgasm, 62–63, 65, 108, 117
otherness, 127
  trauma of, 159

paranoid–schizoid position, 15, 87,
    89–90, 98–99
parent(al), 5, 57, 62, 67, 125, 130, 139,
    147 see also: love
  adoptive, 130

analytical, 29
  couples, 130
  -hood, 151
  images, 130
Pasolini, P., 39–40, 42
Perelberg, R., 89
Persephone, 68, 94–96, 98
perversion, 125
Peskin, H., 15
phallic, 75, 126
  acts, 75
  castration, 117, 125
  desire, 124, 126
  power, 117
  revenge, 73
  self-sufficiency, 81
  strivings, 106
phantasy, 24, 31, 68, 71 see also:
    unconscious(ness), woman
  feminine, 68, 71
  Medea, 68
  of murdering mother, xiv, 68
  of pregnancy, 31
Pines, D., 2
Plato, 153, 156–158
pleasure principle, 153
Pontalis, J.-B., 58
pregnancy, 5, 7–12, 14, 23–24, 54, 62,
    64–71, 79
  ectopic, 7
  interruption, 15–16
  termination, 10, 12, 18
pride, 55, 75, 80–81, 90
primal scene, 2, 109, 112, 117,
    122–123
projection, 2, 23–24, 35, 131, 145–146,
    159
projective identification, 28, 131
psychic(al), 8, 15, 70, 78, 145
    see also: death, trauma,
    violence
  apparatus, 162
  conflict, 53, 149
  de-investment, 58
  determination, 125

energy, 88
flexibility, 71
functioning, 15–16
health, 16
history, 125
imperative, 2
impotence of men, 156
inferiority, 29
maturity, 54
movement, 108
normality, 18
presence, 8
problems, 79
reality, 18
right, 100
situation, 15
solutions, 53
structure, 148, 157
well-being, 71
work, 145, 158
wounds, 80
psychoanalysis, xiv, 3–4, 6, 8, 10, 16,
    18, 26, 28, 30, 45, 57, 64, 76, 110,
    125, 157, 160–164
psychopathic, 41
psychosis, 58
Purhonen, M., 4
Pystynen, T., 100

Quinodoz, J.-M., 2

rage, xiv–xv, 2–3, 7, 39, 53, 67, 72,
    74, 78, 80, 105, 113, 130,
    143–144
Raz, A., 17
reality, 16, 28, 32, 34, 41, 93, 98, 147,
    162, 164, 167
    external, 4, 15–16
    inner, 16
    psychic, 18
Rechardt, E., 58, 75, 86, 88, 157
Reenkola, E., 57–59, 63–64, 66, 68–69,
    71, 76, 104
repetition, 142
    blind, 165

compulsion, 167
    of the trauma, 145
repression, 2, 41, 45, 121, 154–155,
    164
Ricoeur, P., xiii–xiv, 160
Rieder, I., 125
Riedesser, P., 15
Ringler, M., 17
Roos, E., 60, 162–163, 166
Roos, P., 40
Rusconi-Serpa, S., 4

sadism, 56, 59, 62–63, 73–74, 88, 105,
    107
Sandler, A.-M., 2, 148
Sandler, J., 2, 148
Schechter, D., 4
Schück, H., 44
Segal, H., 121
self, 2, 6, 18, 26, 56, 58–59, 63, 75, 80,
    87, 90, 113, 124, 144, 146,
    165–167 see also: defence,
    development(al)
  -accusations, 67
  -analysis, 160
  -blame, 79
  -centred, 61, 80
  -confidence, 32, 49, 63, 66
  -contentedness, 80
  -destruction, 67, 82
  -esteem, 27, 55
  -expression, 95
  evident, 152
  female, 8
  -fulfilment, 78
  grandiose, 104
  ideal, 75, 119, 121, 125
  -image, 17, 142, 160
  murderous, 16
  -object(ive), 159
  -observing, 145
  omnipotent, 121
  -preservation, 56, 59, 155–156
  -punishment, 56, 69
  -reflection, 89

-representation, 1, 87, 90
-respect, 42–43
-righteous, 159
-sacrifice, 78
sense of, 166
-sufficient, 54, 81, 166
whole, 87
separateness, xv, 59, 62–63, 66, 82,
    103–104, 106, 108, 122–123, 127,
    166
sexual, 8, 86, 127, 155 *see also*: couple,
    development(al), drive, fantasy,
    instinct, life, love, woman
abuse, 161
adult, 57
bi-, 124
body, 91
characters, 125
crimes, 56
current of feelings, 156
desire, 59, 64, 70, 107–109
dimension, 62
energy, 55, 61, 155
experience, 65
function, 58
gratification, 167
hetero-, 124, 127
homo-, 125
inhibitions, 65
interest, 109
libido, 61, 155
    homo-, 107, 124
partner, 107
passion, 2, 15, 60, 109, 153
pleasure, 71, 109
preference, 157
relationship, 78–79, 109, 117, 120
    homo-, 121
roles, 65
satisfaction, 108, 123, 155, 159
system, 156
union, 62
sexuality, 7, 56, 64–65, 77, 153,
    156–157
bi-, 124

cruel, 56
Freudian, 156
homo-, 124
    female, 124
human, 154, 159
infantile, 153
narcissistic, 159
psycho-, 153
repressed, 121
theme, 6
Shakespeare, W., 41, 60, 154, 165
    Romeo and Juliet, 60, 165
shame, xv, 23, 25, 55, 67, 69–70,
    72–75, 77–82, 89, 95, 100, 104,
    110, 120, 122–123, 126–127, 144,
    146
Shook, J. J., 86
sibling rivalry, 103
Singer, L., 167
Södergran, E., xv, 104, 107, 110–118,
    120, 127
Solomon, E. P., 86
somatisation, 135
Sophocles, 44, 161
Spielrein, S., 57–58
split, 32, 53, 87, 97, 100, 122–123, 125,
    149, 154–156
    -off, 2, 4, 17, 77, 108
    profound, 1
    psychic, 15
Stein, N., 86
Stendhal, 152
sterility
    desolation of, 29
    psychogenic, 15
Stern, D., 4
subject(ive), 41, 57, 72, 88, 126, 144,
    157, 159, 165–167
    feeling, 59
    inter-, 18
    nature, xv, 151
    of reflection, 9
    whole, 87
sublimation, xv, 127
symbiotic fusion, 67, 106, 110 .

symbol(ic), 2, 42, 58–59, 68, 70,
    105–109, 112, 117, 121, 123, 126,
    166
  exploration, xiv
  matricide, 56–57
  of evil, 99
  power, 124
  value, 126
symptoms, 6

Tambelli, R., 4
Tarachow, S., xiii
Target, M., 89
Teising, M., 2, 9–10
tender(ness), xiv, 36, 42, 44, 46, 62,
    70, 74, 106–107, 115, 155, 162,
    166
Thanatos, 58, 86, 99, 109, 157
  see also: death
Toedter, L. J., 17
Tognoli Pasquali, L., 50
Tolstoy, L. N., 37, 43, 165
  Anna Karenina, 43, 165
tragedy, xiii, 25–27, 32, 40–41, 44–45,
    47–48, 95, 160
transference, 2, 7, 17, 38, 71, 104,
    131, 143, 167 *see also*:
    countertransference
  erotic, 106
  female, 33
  history of, 154
  love, 164
  negative, 124
  situations, 1
  twinship, 104
transformation, 159, 161
transition(al), 61, 127
  object, 122, 167
  phenomena, 104, 127
  space, 106
  state, 108–109, 122
trauma(tic), 4, 10, 15–18, 67, 130,
    133, 136, 143–145, 154, 159
  see also: mother
  activated, 134

acute, 16
adult, 145
attachment, 86
dramatic, 17
event, 18, 145
experience, 4, 14, 144–145
indicator, 135
infantile, 145
linking, 134
manifestations, 149
memories, 139, 145
psychic(al), 144
quality, 8, 18
reactions, xv, 130–131, 145
separation, 139, 166
severe, 3
situation, 15, 18
Trentini, C., 4
truth, 4, 24, 30, 60, 135, 146, 152, 158,
    162–164
Tsiantis, J., 2, 9, 15, 17–18
Tustin, F., 146, 148

unconscious(ness), xiii, 2, 4, 7, 16, 18,
    27, 35, 68, 78, 80, 92–93, 95–96,
    108–109, 111, 123, 156, 159, 165,
    167 *see also*: aggression/
    aggressive, anger,
    conscious(ness), defence,
    world
  aggression, 147–148
  aim, 163
  anger, 15, 144
  archaic world, 16
  belief, 2
  conflicts, 4
  conviction, 2
  dynamic, 2
  enactment, 2
  fantasy, xiii, 1, 8, 10, 16, 96
    Medea, xiv, 1, 4, 7, 15, 17
    sister, 122
  fears, 109, 159
  female truth, 4
  feminine self-image, 17

human, 98
image, 99
issues, 4
layers of the mind, 48
level, 69
perception, 166
personal, 28
phantasy, 68, 71
projections, 2
psychological motives, 65
revenge, 124
wish, xiii, 85
    baby, 66
    death, 69

Valkonen-Korhonen, M., 4
value, 28, 32, 49, 63, 78, 81, 98, 152,
    157, 160, 162 *see also*: woman
instrumental, 152
intrinsic, 152
of truth, 163
symbolic, 126
Varvin, S., 148
violence, 27, 32, 59, 81, 85–86, 88–89,
    94–95, 99–100
mental, 54, 56, 78
physical, 54, 56, 78
psychic(al), 59
social, 95
virtue, 92, 152, 162–163
Voigt, D., 125
Von Trier, L., 37, 41–43, 45–48, 50
vulnerability, 9, 55, 80–81, 90, 149
in-, 8
mental, 49
narcissistic, 145

Waddell, M., 147–148
Waelder, R., 167
Wallace, J. M., 86
war child, xv, 129–131, 133, 135, 140,
    146, 148–149
Wertz, D. D., 17
Wharton, B., 57
whore, 46, 156

Widlöcher, D., 153
Wilde, O., 164
Winnicott, D. W., 56–57, 59, 61–62,
    113, 120, 122, 130, 144
wish, 69–70, 75, 78–79, 87, 93, 100,
    111, 115, 139, 142, 159–160, 165,
    see also: aggression/aggressive,
    unconscious(ness)
baby, 66
children's, 57, 123
death, 67–69, 71, 82
fairy-tale, 16
for a child, 65, 90
for motherhood, 65
for revenge, 38
for termination of pregnancy, 66
-fulfilling, 162
images, 166
murderous, 40
of the id, 167
pregnancy, 68
thinking, 163
woman
abandoned, 23
aggression/aggressive, 59, 94
and cancer, 13
and child, 65–66, 75
and pregnancy, 10, 47, 54, 68–69, 79
at war with self, xiv, 36
barbarian, 72
evil, 93
fertility, 68, 71, 96
heart, 43
homosexual, 124
-hood, xiii
ideals, 75–76, 81
identity, 36
image of, 90, 125
in relationships, xiv, 26–27, 36, 62,
    85, 117, 125
inferiority of, 29
intelligent, 25
older, 70
phantasy, 71
proud, 21, 29, 55, 80–81

psyche, 76
psychic
   flexibility, 71
   maturity, 54
   right to decide, 69
sexual
   desire, 107, 112, 117, 124
   inhibitions, 65
sexually active, 8
shamed, 81
successful, 79
timid, 72
value, 78
vengeance, 92, 95
victim, 56
wise, 92–94
world, xiv
wounded, 27
young, xv, 6
Woolf, V., 28
world *see also*: woman
   adult, 50
   archaic, 16

depressed, 35
developed, 39
external, 56, 61, 159
fantasy, 1
frightening, 147
hostile, 21
inner, 39, 42, 111, 148, 165
magical, 30
masculine, 42, 49–50
of ancient tragedy, 40
of phenomena, 40
of power, 42
of the immortals, 47
other person's, xiv, 35
outside, 5, 87, 148
phobic, 6
separate, 39
subterranean, 98
unconscious(ness), 4, 16
under-, 95, 98–99
Wortis, J., 163

Young-Bruehl, E., 119–121

For Product Safety Concerns and Information please contact our EU
representative GPSR@taylorandfrancis.com
Taylor & Francis Verlag GmbH, Kaufingerstraße 24, 80331 München, Germany

www.ingramcontent.com/pod-product-compliance
Lightning Source LLC
Chambersburg PA
CBHW070422270326
41926CB00014B/2895